She Dared

—◆◆◆—

TRUE STORIES OF HEROINES, SCOUNDRELS, AND RENEGADES

ED BUTTS

Illustrated by Heather Collins

Tundra Books

Text copyright © 2005 by Ed Butts
Illustrations copyright © 2005 by Heather Collins

Published in Canada by Tundra Books,
481 University Avenue, Toronto, Ontario M5G 2E9

Published in the United States by Tundra Books of Northern New York,
P.O. Box 1030, Plattsburgh, New York 12901

Library of Congress Control Number: 2004110127

Library and Archives Canada Cataloguing in Publication

Butts, Edward, 1951–
She dared : true stories of heroines, scoundrels, and renegades / Ed Butts ; illustrated by Heather Collins.

Includes bibliographical references.
ISBN 0-88776-718-4

1. Women–Canada–Biography–Juvenile literature.
2. Canada–Biography–Juvenile literature. I. Collins, Heather II. Title.

FC26.W6B88 2005   j920.72'0971   C2004-904125-8

We acknowledge the financial support of the Government of Canada through the Book Publishing Industry Development Program (BPIDP) and that of the Government of Ontario through the Ontario Media Development Corporation's Ontario Book Initiative. We further acknowledge the support of the Canada Council for the Arts and the Ontario Arts Council for our publishing program.

The illustrations for this book were rendered in graphite.

Design: Cindy Reichle

Printed in Canada

1 2 3 4 5 6   10 09 08 07 06 05

For my mother, Patricia; my sisters, Eileen, Deborah,
and Patrice; and my daughter, Melanie
E.B.

For Blair, who has always encouraged me to dare
H.C.

Acknowledgments

The author would like to thank the public libraries of Toronto and Guelph, Ontario; the Public Archives of Canada, the Archives of Ontario, the Hudson's Bay Company Archives; and Shirley Render of Winnipeg, Manitoba.

Contents

Introduction

History has often overlooked women. Browse through any encyclopedia, and it is obvious that the biographical sketches are overwhelmingly the stories of men. It is as though women, with a few outstanding exceptions, have had relatively little to contribute in the various fields of human endeavor.

One of the main reasons for this unfortunate situation is that for centuries women were overlooked *in* history. It was not that women did not have the potential to be great artists, politicians, philosophers, or even soldiers. It was that they were not given the opportunities. For centuries it was generally accepted – by men and women alike – that women were not capable of doing "a man's work." Women were believed to be physically, mentally, and emotionally inferior to men. The father was the head of the household. Wives owed obedience to their husbands. Sons were heirs ahead of daughters. While we, looking back from the 21st century, might condemn all this as terribly unfair, it would be wrong of us to judge our ancestors. Everything in their social environment – culture, religion, and philosophy – supported the system.

Women were not *expected* to step beyond the bounds of convention. Their place was where their society told them it was, and that was usually in the home. A lady of the nobility may have enjoyed greater wealth, comfort, and leisure time than a peasant woman, but she was just as much restricted by the moral and social codes of her time.

Of course, there were women who dared to challenge those codes. They did so at the risk of stirring up public anger, creating scandal, estranging their families, even breaking the law. Some did it for personal, even self-centered reasons. Others were motivated by ideals of social justice.

This volume presents the stories of 15 women of Canada who dared in some way to challenge their societies. They ventured into areas previously considered off-limits to females – medicine, publishing, the military. They survived harrowing ordeals and courted forbidden romance. Some were Canadian born; others came to Canada from elsewhere. They emerged from different backgrounds, but their common bond was daring to step off the narrow path of custom. Some of these women made mistakes and engaged in criminal activities, for which they paid the price. What they did was not admirable, but like the women whose accomplishments were nobler, they, too, are part of history.

She Dared

TRUE STORIES OF
HEROINES, SCOUNDRELS,
AND RENEGADES

1

Marguerite de la Roque de Roberval

Survivor in a Strange Land

One hundred and seventy-five years before Daniel Defoe wrote his famous novel *Robinson Crusoe*, there was an even more dramatic castaway story unfolding off the coast of Newfoundland. This one was not the result of stormy seas, but of forbidden love.

Marguerite de la Roque de Roberval was a young girl from an old, upper-class French family and was a relative, likely a niece, of Jean François de la Rocque de Roberval. Jean François was a flamboyant man who was forever running into trouble. He had financial problems and had borrowed heavily from his relatives, perhaps even from young Marguerite. He had sailed as a privateer and seized English ships, angering King Henry VIII of England. And he was a French Protestant at a time when the Roman Catholic majority in France felt Protestants should be hanged. Luckily he was a personal friend of Prince François, who would later be king, and that saved him. The French ruler pretended to be angry with Roberval, while all the time keeping him on as a friend at court.

In 1540 Roberval hatched an idea. He decided that he could regain his fortunes and earn immortal glory by establishing a colony in Canada, the territory "discovered" just a few years earlier by Jacques Cartier. The French were jealous of all the gold and silver that the Spanish were looting from their New World Empire in Mexico and South America, and hoped that Canada might hold similar riches. Cartier had partially navigated the St. Lawrence River and had heard stories from the Natives that convinced him there were precious metals and gems farther up the great river in a place called Saguenay. The French also believed that the St. Lawrence might provide a passage through the New World to the Pacific Ocean – a trade route to China. The French king happily bought in to Roberval's idea and made him "Lieutenant-General of the country of Canada." Cartier was appointed second-in-command. This did not go over at all well with Cartier. As the discoverer of the new territory, he had expected to lead a colonizing expedition himself. It made him furious to be reduced to the position of mere guide for a courtier. It probably bewildered him, too, that a Protestant such as Roberval (who may have temporarily rejoined the Catholics) should be given the mission of "spreading the holy Catholic faith" to the Natives.

By May of 1541, Cartier was ready to go with a fleet of five ships, but Roberval had been having difficulties raising funds and recruiting colonists. As a result, Cartier sailed on ahead, agreeing to meet his 'commander' in Canada.

It took another whole year for Roberval to outfit and supply his three ships: the *Anne*, the *Valentine*, and the *Lechefraye*. To make up for a shortage in manpower, he had to drag convicted murderers and thieves out of prisons. It was quite common in those times to use prisoners for the hard, dirty, dangerous jobs that no one else wanted. Sailing off into the Great Unknown on a crowded little ship was certainly one of those jobs. A sailor's life was tough at the best of times, but for those who embarked on these early trans-Atlantic voyages, it was a downright miserable ordeal of hard work, bad food, and the lash.

The voyage was somewhat more bearable for the aristocrats on board – the gentlemen who were to be the pillars of society in the new colony – and their ladies. One of the women invited to go on the adventure was Roberval's niece, Marguerite. She was a member of his household and, according to reports of the time, Roberval treated her like a daughter. As a

rule, girls of the upper class were married off at a very young age.
Marguerite was still single, so quite likely she was young, perhaps in her
midteens. We know that she was a young woman of some financial means.
Marguerite was coseigneuress – with Roberval – of an estate northeast of
Paris and had property of her own at Perigord and Languedoc to the south.
She was probably in a position to lend her uncle money for his expedition.

Marguerite must have been a spirited girl to set off on an expedition
across the sea and into the wilds of Canada, even under the care of a loving
uncle. She certainly wouldn't have been trained to cope with a rough
lifestyle. Highborn French ladies of that time were raised to be delicate,
charming creatures who would look pretty at a husband's side, and who
knew all the etiquette of the ballroom, the salon, and the dining room.
They most definitely did not work. There were servants for that. But
Roberval must have known that Marguerite had more strength in her than
the average young woman when he took her along on the voyage. What
he did not know when his small fleet set sail from La Rochelle on
April 16, 1542, was that little Mademoiselle Marguerite already had a
lover! And on top of that shocking fact was something just as scandalous.
He was not a gentleman of her social status, but a lowly commoner.

The name of the handsome young man who volunteered to sail with
Roberval is not known, but according to one report, "(he) came more for
the love of the *damoiselle* than for the service of the King or respect for the
Captain." From this it is safe to assume that the relationship had been going
on for some time. Obviously Marguerite had a mind of her own if she
became romantically involved with a commoner, but strong-willed or not,
she had to keep the love affair a secret. Ladies of the time simply did not
mix with the lower classes. A male aristocrat might spend time with a
lower class woman for his own amusement, though he would never marry
beneath his station; but for a female aristocrat to become overly familiar
with a lower class man was absolutely taboo. Even among their social
equals, aristocratic girls were expected to behave according to a strict code
of conduct. Marriages had to be approved by parents or legal guardians and

more often than not were arranged by heads of families. The girl rarely had any say in the choice of her husband. Marguerite was playing with fire.

Roberval's fleet was delayed by bad winds right away and it wasn't until June 8, 1542 that the *Anne,* the *Valentine,* and the *Lechefraye* dropped anchor in the port of St. John's, Newfoundland. So far, Marguerite and her lover had managed to keep their affair a secret. Probably the only other person who knew of it was Damienne, Marguerite's trusted servant.

Though Roberval did not yet know of his niece's indiscretion, other problems made him surly and short-tempered. The delays during the ocean crossing had been maddening enough. Now he found himself in the middle of a dispute between French and Portuguese fishermen at St. John's. The fishing fleets of several nations gathered annually to harvest the cod of Newfoundland's legendary Grand Banks, and there were frequently quarrels among the rival crews. The disputes, plus the time needed to restock his vessels with fresh water, cost Roberval another three weeks. To top it all off, Cartier arrived from the St. Lawrence and impudently announced that he was heading back to France.

Roberval ordered the explorer to return to Canada with him. Cartier reluctantly agreed, but then slipped away under cover of darkness the first chance he got, and sailed for France. His ship was full of what he thought were gold and diamonds and he didn't want Roberval grabbing the glory for this great find. As it turned out, his "gold" was iron pyrite – fool's gold – and his "diamonds" were nothing but quartz.

Marguerite and her young man took advantage of the stopover at St. John's to escape the cramped quarters of the ship and spend some time together – out of the sight of her uncle. Damienne was their lookout. They strolled along the wild Newfoundland shore, climbed the hills behind St. John's, picked blueberries, and fished the streams for salmon. It was spring and for two young people in love, this beautiful corner of the New World, far from the smothering restrictions of France, must have seemed an enchanting place. Perhaps their happiness made them careless. Somehow, Marguerite's uncle discovered their secret.

Roberval was furious. Not only was Marguerite being unladylike, but she also had broken one of the strictest rules of her social class. She was consorting with a man who was by far her inferior – a nobody! She had disgraced herself, brought shame to her noble family name, and insulted the dignity of her uncle. To Roberval, Marguerite was the guiltier of the two. She was an aristocrat and should have known better. The young man was but an ignorant peasant. If Roberval had discovered the affair while they were still in France, he probably would have had the poor youth flogged and driven from the estate. Marguerite likely would have been banished to a convent and a life of penance under the watchful eyes of nuns.

But there were no convents in Newfoundland. The punishment Roberval ultimately decided upon was drastic, even for him, and he was a harsh commander indeed. Shortly after leaving St. John's, Roberval abandoned his niece, her lover, and the servant Damienne on an uninhabited island.

Most historians believe it was Fogo Island off the northeast coast of Newfoundland, but some think it could have been in the Strait of Belle Isle or in the Gulf of St. Lawrence. Mariners thought the island was haunted, and called it Isle of Demons. One account of the incident says that Roberval first ordered only the young man to be put on the island, and that Marguerite begged to join him. The other version of the story claims that it was Marguerite who was being marooned, and that the young man voluntarily went with her. Damienne might have accompanied Marguerite out of loyalty to her mistress, or maybe Roberval sent the servant to her doom because he considered her guilty for helping to keep the affair secret.

Roberval was pleased that he could punish the offenders without staining his hands with their blood, but for all intents and purposes he had served them with a death sentence. Without proper provisions, Europeans had a very poor chance of survival in the North American wilderness. Being confined to an island, with no way of reaching the mainland, made the situation even more desperate. Perhaps Roberval expected fishermen would find the trio and rescue them. There certainly is no record that he ever sent anyone back to the island or made any inquiries as to the fate of his niece and her companions.

The castaways were left in an alien place where, for most of the year, the climate was hostile to those who did not know how to cope with it. They had a few clothes, some tools, and four arquebuses (a type of matchlock gun) with some gunpowder and shot. Anything else they needed to keep themselves alive, they would have to find on the island.

The first summer was as comfortable as could be expected. At first they slept outside in the rain and chilling fog under a crude shelter of leaves, but they soon built a log hut and made beds of cedar boughs. No doubt keeping an eye on the ocean horizon for any sign of a sail, they gathered birds' eggs, collected berries and other fruit, and caught fish. There were rabbits, deer, bears, and beaver on the island, as well as numerous sea birds. These they shot or snared for meat and furs to make into clothing and bedding. Marguerite probably learned a lot about the day-to-day tasks of looking after oneself from her young lover and her servant. But her strength and unwavering determination to stay alive seems to have come from within herself.

The little house protected them from the elements and a fire kept them warm, but at night they huddled in terror of the ghosts and demons they thought were lurking in the woods. Strange shrieks and cries pierced the night. These were likely the calls of unfamiliar birds and animals. As the season progressed and the wild night sounds decreased, Marguerite believed that their strong Christian faith had driven the evil spirits away. In truth, the noisy migratory birds had simply flown south, since winter was approaching. Also gone, with the approach of cold weather, was any hope of rescue for many months.

Winter off the coast of Newfoundland is long, cold, and bleak. To the three souls stranded on the island it must have seemed that they were the only people in the world. Every day brought the monotonous but necessary chores of hauling firewood and finding food. Then Marguerite became pregnant, and as she grew bigger she found it awkward to forage for food and fuel. Her young man fell into a state of depression and nothing the two women did could help him. The youth, who had so gallantly joined an expedition so he could be with his heart's true love, apparently gave up all hope. He died before a grief-stricken Marguerite gave birth to their baby daughter. Now it was up to Marguerite to provide for herself, the child, and Damienne.

Meanwhile, things were not going well for Roberval, hundreds of miles away on the banks of the St. Lawrence. His colony at Cap Rouge, near today's Québec City, was hit by cold, sickness, starvation, and mutiny. The local Natives, suspicious of the French colonists' reasons for being in their country, would not come to Roberval's settlement to trade, making it all the more difficult for the hungry settlers to obtain food. Fifty settlers died of scurvy. Others were flogged whenever Roberval felt their work was not up to his expectations, or when they were charged with petty theft. Some were even placed in leg irons and banished to an island. One day Roberval had six men hanged. Even though Roberval had to maintain firm control over the many convicts he had obtained from French jails, he was more than firm – he was extremely cruel.

Roberval returned to France in 1543. His colonizing venture was such an utter failure that two generations would pass before France would make another attempt to plant a settlement in Canada.

If Marguerite had known that her uncle had departed from the New World, never to return, she might well have given up all hope of ever leaving the Isle of Demons alive. But she didn't know, and she struggled to live. She learned to use the arquebus well, even though it was awkward to handle. She had to be very careful with her supply of gunpowder, because once it was gone there was no replacing it. Nonetheless, she was able to bring down bears with her gun and once she killed a bear "as white as an egg" – a polar bear that had come with the ice-pans floating down from the North.

But for all her hard work and determination, Marguerite could not stop tragedy from striking again. Sixteen or seventeen months after Roberval had left her on the island, Marguerite could only look on in helpless grief as Damienne and the baby – barely a year old – died from illness or malnutrition. She buried them beside her lost young man, and then she was all alone. Another dreadful year would pass before she would look at another human face or hear a human voice other than her own.

The loneliness must have been crushing. Day after day passed with no one to talk to but the animals, no comforting hand or reassuring voice when she was ill or afraid. She shuddered at the awful thought that if she died, there would be no one to give her a Christian burial. Marguerite's Christianity was important to her. She had christened her baby herself, and quite likely she and her lover had carried out some form of simple ceremony to make their union holy before God. Now she prayed to God as she began to experience visions – "stranger than man could imagine" – that were probably hallucinations brought on by her weakened mental and physical state. On a few occasions in that horrible year Marguerite spotted sails on the horizon, but each time they disappeared without coming near the Isle of Demons. Her heart sank, even as her mind told her that the sailors would have no desire to approach such a haunted place.

Then one momentous day in the autumn of 1545, two years and five months after she had been marooned, Marguerite saw a fleet of ships just off her island prison. Marguerite lit a signal fire, then ran down to the shore, shouting, jumping, and waving to attract attention. The sailors were French cod fishermen, and at first they were afraid. After all, this was the Isle of Demons! What could that wild looking thing dressed in animal skins be but some kind of a devil? From where she danced frantically on the shore, it looked to Marguerite as if they were going to flee from her in fear. Then what could she look forward to but another long, lonely winter – if she survived at all.

But someone in one of the boats had second thoughts. Perhaps one fisherman was a little braver than the others, or a little less superstitious. Perhaps someone recognized her voice as being human. Perhaps one of them realized that demons don't light signal fires. A small boat cautiously approached the shore, and the astonished men in it saw that the shaggy-looking "demon" was actually a French woman. Marguerite was saved! She showed the men the hut that had been her home for almost two-and-a-half years, and the graves of her child, her servant, and the man she had loved. Then emotion overcame her. She wept and said that she could not bear to leave the three people she loved more dearly than anyone else in the world. She wanted to stay and die on the island. The fishermen finally persuaded her it would be better for her to return home with them. She knew they were right.

Marguerite sailed with the fishing fleet back to La Rochelle in France, where three years earlier she had set off on an adventure with the uncle she thought had loved her, and the man with whom she was in love. There she was "received with great honour by all the women" who were amazed at her story. She eventually told her tale to André Thevet, a priest who was one of the earliest historians of French Canada. Marguerite de Navarre, sister of the king and an acquaintance of Roberval, also wrote an account of the story.

There is no record that Marguerite and her uncle ever met again. She had been a person of property when she left France to accompany him on his expedition, but she might have lost the estates when she was presumed dead. She filled her days by running a school for girls in La Rochelle, but whether she did so out of financial need or just to contribute something to the community is not certain. She did whisper from time to time that she wished she were back on the island with her three loved ones.

While Marguerite lived a quiet life at the school, her uncle's life continued on its unfortunate path to doom. In 1560, as he and some fellow Protestants were leaving a meeting in Paris, they were attacked by assassins and murdered. Creditors seized whatever property Roberval still owned. His only legacies were debt and failure. But the niece he had so callously abandoned on a forlorn island became one of Canada's first heroines. She had dared to follow her heart into forbidden love, and survived – against all odds – on a lonely little island in the midst of a cold and forbidding sea.

2

Thanadelthur

The Woman Who Stopped a War

To the Native peoples who lived in the rugged Canadian North in the 17th and 18th centuries, the European notion that women were the "weaker sex" was a joke. Native women were an important part of the work force, and helped keep the economy going. Men hunted large game, but once an animal was killed, every step in the process of turning it into food, clothing, and tools was done by the women. Even hunting wasn't an exclusively male task. Women snared small game like rabbits and birds, food sources that were vital to a tribe's survival when large game was scarce. Women also tended fishing nets, gathered roots and wild rice, and did all the agricultural work. On the trail, Native women carried heavier loads than men, and on the water they were expert paddlers.

With the coming of the white fur traders, Native women proved themselves vital to the fur trade economy because they dressed the pelts. The white traders learned, sometimes slowly, that their business simply could not thrive without Native women. Expeditions sent inland to trade or explore most often failed if they weren't accompanied by women.

There was more to it than back-breaking work. The white traders found that women could have considerable influence on the decisions made by the male leaders of their tribes. White men began taking Native wives – a practice often frowned upon by their company superiors. From their wives white traders learned Native languages and dialects. Moreover, a white trader with a Native wife immediately had family connections among the tribal clans, which could be valuable. Native women could be very effective negotiators, and in Canada's wild north country, a young Chipewyan named Thanadelthur was the most outstanding female diplomat.

Thanadelthur, whose name has been translated as "Jumping Marten" or "Marten Shake," was born to the Slave clan of the Chipewyan, probably in the Great Slave Lake area, about 1697. The term "slave" did not necessarily have anything to do with servitude. It was a name given to a generally peaceful people by their more aggressive Cree rivals. According to Chipewyan legend, at the time she played her part in history Thanadelthur was young – perhaps not yet 20 – and beautiful.

Thanadelthur lived during a time of upheaval. The Cree had direct contact with French and English traders on Hudson Bay, and from them had acquired guns. The Cree used these powerful new weapons to dominate nearby tribes, including the Chipewyan. The Cree developed their own trade networks, bartering goods they had obtained from the whites to other tribes at greatly inflated prices. They also blocked the others from the trading posts. When the Europeans wanted to travel inland to make contact with other tribes, the Cree warned them off with wild tales of fierce warriors and cannibals. The Cree also raided into the territories of other tribes, whose bows and arrows were of little use against guns.

On one of these raids, in the spring of 1713, young Thanadelthur was seized and carried off into captivity. Ironically, because she was a woman she was not killed, and later was able to play her amazing role in the story of the North.

Thanadelthur spent about a year with the Cree as a real slave. But she learned the Cree language and saw that her captors had many useful items they had acquired in trade from the whites, whom they called the "Stone House People." There were steel knives and hatchet blades, metal scrapers for dressing hides, cooking kettles and ice-chisels, cloth, blankets, as well as the lovely beads and ribbons the girls and women liked so much.

Thanadelthur might have seen some of these items before, but they were expensive for her people because they could only be purchased from Cree middlemen. She figured that if the Chipewyan could trade directly with the Stone House People, they, too, could have these luxuries – which would be a blessing to the hardworking women. Even more importantly, they could get guns to defend themselves against the marauding Cree.

One day in the fall of 1714, Thanadelthur and another Chipewyan woman escaped. It was a daring move. Recapture would mean severe punishment, perhaps even death. With no food except what they could catch in their snares, the two women tried to make their way across country to their own land before winter set in. But cold, snow, and hunger forced them to turn back. Their only hope lay in finding the Stone House People before their Cree masters could catch them again. Thanadelthur had never seen white people before, but she was sure she and her friend would find shelter with the people who had made all the wonderful things she had seen in the Cree village. When Thanadelthur's companion died, probably from starvation, Thanadelthur pressed on alone. She came upon some tracks in the snow and followed them. By good fortune, she walked into a camp of goose hunters from the Hudson's Bay Company post of York Factory. As fate would have it, she had made her acquaintance with 'The Honourable Company,' as the English liked to call it, at a very dramatic moment.

For several years there had been on-and-off warfare around the shores of Hudson Bay, as the French and the English battled over control of the fur trade. York Factory had been captured by the French in 1697. They lost it under the 1713 Treaty of Utrecht, which said it had to be returned to the Hudson's Bay Company. Governor James Knight, a tough, veteran Company man in his mid-70s, had just taken command in 1714, and was trying to re-establish trade for the English.

It would not be easy. The Native people complained – with good reason – that the French trade goods, especially their guns, were better than the English ones. The French still had a trading post on the Albany River, and were intercepting a lot of trade that might otherwise have gone to York Factory. Governor Knight didn't have the manpower to drive the French from their post, but he wanted to increase business at York by opening up new territory to the north and west. The problem was that the northern Natives – including the Chipewyan and the Cree – were constantly at war. War was bad for business. Natives on the warpath did not take the time to trap furs. Not only that, the northern Natives were afraid to cross Cree territory to get to York Factory. Knight had to find a way to stop the fighting and convince the northern tribes that they could bring their furs to York Factory safely. He would need an interpreter for this, and the only woman at York Factory who spoke Chipewyan had just died. Two days later Thanadelthur walked into the fort with the party of goose hunters.

Knight was not an easy man to impress, but he was quite taken with Thanadelthur, whom he always referred to in his journal as "the Slave Woman." Knight listened in fascination as Thanadelthur told him about her country where there was ". . . abundance of Indians to the Westward and Norward of them & that there is plenty of Marten Ermine fox Wolf Quequihatch (Wolverine) & Buffelow (sic). . . ." She also spoke of a "yellow mettle (sic)" that he thought could be copper or even gold.

Over the winter Thanadelthur convinced the governor that she could persuade the northern tribes to make peace if he could talk the Cree into burying the hatchet. In June 1715, Knight held a great feast for the Cree and presented them with gifts of tobacco, gunpowder, shot, and other trade goods. He made them understand that it would be in their best interests to stop waging war on the northern tribes. He even talked them into sending a peace delegation into Chipewyan country to meet with the chiefs there and make peace.

Two weeks later, 150 Cree set out from York Factory on the peace mission. With them went a Company man, William Stuart, and Thanadelthur, as interpreter. She was to help convince her people that the war was over, and tell them that Knight promised to build them a trading post at the mouth of the Churchill River in a year. Knight instructed

Stuart to ". . . take care that none of the Indians Abuse or Misuse the Slave Woman . . . or take what She has from her that is to be given Amongst her Country people. . . ."

Officially Stuart was the leader of the expedition, but it soon became obvious that the real driving force was Thanadelthur. She knew how important the mission was, but it must have seemed strange to her to be traveling with a large band of Cree, her people's enemies. She made it quite clear, however, that she was not afraid of them. Knight later wrote that Stuart ". . . never See one of Such a Spirit in his Life. She kept all the (Cree) Indians in Awe as she went with and never Spared in telling them of their Cowardly way of Killing her Country Men."

As the peace party made its way in search of the Chipewyan, sickness began to strike and food ran short. In order to survive, the travelers had to break up into smaller groups. Most turned back. One group paused long enough to commit an act that almost wrecked the peace mission. Before Thanadelthur, Stuart, and the Cree could locate the Chipewyan, they came upon the scene of a massacre. Nine Chipewyan Indians lay dead on the ground, victims of one of the other Cree bands. The Cree in Thanadelthur's group were now afraid that the Chipewyan would kill them in revenge. They wanted to abandon the peace mission, but Thanadelthur would have none of it. She told the Cree to camp where they were, and to give her 10 days. She would find her people and bring them back to talk peace. While Stuart and the Cree fortified their camp in case of attack, Thanadelthur set off alone, following the trail of the Chipewyan who had escaped the massacre.

A few days later she found a village of more than 400 of her people. Because of the murder of the nine Chipewyan, it was not easy for Thanadelthur to convince the people that the Cree nation really wanted peace. But she would not take no for an answer. Knight's journal reports that ". . . the woman had made herself so hoarse with her perpetuall (sic) talking to her Country Men in perswadin (sic) them to come with her that Shee (sic) could hardly speak. . . ."

Back at the Cree camp, the 10th day came, and Stuart and the Natives with him were convinced that Thanadelthur had failed. Then, dramatically, she came in sight with two Chipewyan men. When Stuart went out to meet them and invite them into his tent, Thanadelthur gave a hand signal and 160 more Chipewyan appeared. The Cree in the camp must have been trembling in their moccasins, but their leader, with Thanadelthur's help, managed to convince the Chipewyan that these Cree were not responsible for the murder of the nine people. Then they all got down to the business of ending the war.

Stuart and Thanadelthur distributed the gifts they had brought with them, and the Cree said they were willing to smoke the peace pipe with the Chipewyan. Some of the Chipewyan were reluctant to agree to a treaty, but Thanadelthur bullied them into it. Stuart reported to Knight that, "She made them all stand in fear of her. She scolded some and pushing of others . . . and forced them to ye peace." Stuart gave Thanadelthur full credit for the success of the mission, and expressed his admiration for her. "Indeed she has a Devillish (sic) Spirit and I believe that if thare (sic) were but 50 of her Country Men of the Same Carriage and Resolution they would drive all the (Southern) Indians in America out of there (sic) Country."

Thanadelthur's party returned in triumph to York Factory in May 1716, almost 10 months after they had set out. With them were 10 Chipewyan, including Thanadelthur's own brother. Knight was more than pleased with the success of the mission and reported to his superiors that the person most responsible for that success was "the Slave Woman."

Thanadelthur married a Chipewyan man, but told Knight that she would be willing to travel throughout the north country, sending Natives to him with their furs and explaining to her people that the promised post at Churchill would be delayed because the supply ship was late. She even said that if her husband would not go with her, she would leave him.

Knight admired the "Extraordinary Vivacity" of Thanadelthur's mind, and sought her advice as he made plans to expand the Company trade. She began to learn English. As Chipewyans came in during that summer and fall of 1716, she instructed them on how to cure their furs for trade purposes. When one of her own people suggested that low quality furs could be passed off with the good ones, she "ketcht him by the nose, pushed him backwards, and called him a fool," according to Knight.

On one occasion her friend Governor Knight got a taste of Thanadelthur's temper. He had lectured her for giving away a kettle he had given her as a gift. Knight said, "She did rise in such a passion as I never did see the like before." In her fury, she told the old governor that if he ever set foot north of the Churchill River, she would order her people to kill him. Knight responded by cuffing her ears. The next day Thanadelthur begged Knight's forgiveness for her outburst. She said that he was like a father to her, and that all Natives loved him.

Knight was especially interested in Thanadelthur's stories about the people who had the "yellow mettle." She promised to show him where it could be found, but early in 1717 several of the Chipewyans at York Factory, including Thanadelthur, fell ill. On January 11 Knight wrote in his journal, "Ye Northern Slave Woman has been dangerously Ill and I expect her Death every Day, but I hope she is now a Recovering."

Thanadelthur did not recover, in spite of Knight's efforts to nurse her back to health. On February 5, a grieving Knight wrote, ". . . this morning the Northern Slave Woman departed her Life after About Seven Weeks Illness . . . She was one of a Very high Spirit and of the Firmest Resolution that ever I see in any Body in my Days and of Great Courage & forecast . . . I am almost ready to break my heart."

Knight had not just lost his Chipewyan interpreter, he also had lost a good friend. As promised, he built a Hudson's Bay Company post at the mouth of the Churchill River (now the site of Churchill, Manitoba) later that year. He went back to England, and two years later, at the age of 80, set sail once more to look for a Northwest Passage and the "yellow mettle." Knight, his two ships, and all of his men vanished forever in the Arctic mist. Knight's disappearance was the closing chapter in the legendary story of Thanadelthur, the young Chipewyan woman whose daring stopped a war.

3

Molly Brant

The Voice of Two Worlds

Molly Brant was born about 1736 on the banks of the Ohio River and given the Mohawk name *Degonwadonti* (Many Against One). When her father died, her mother took 10-year-old Molly and her little brother *Thayendanega* (Two Sticks of Wood Bound Together) to the Mohawk town called Canajohari Castle. There they lived with a relative, Nickus Brant. The children's English names were Mary and Joseph, but Mary was most commonly called Miss Molly.

The Mohawks – along with the Senecas, Onondagas, Oneidas, Cayugas, and Tuscaroras – were part of the Iroquois Six Nations Confederacy. This organization of tribes had considerable political and miliatary power. The people were farmers and hunters who had traditionally lived in villages of longhouses, though by Molly's time they lived in homes like the ones built by European settlers.

Iroquois society was matrilineal, which means that bloodlines are traced through the mother's side of the family. Women owned most of the property and controlled the agricultural food supply. Moreover, women had political power. It was the women who selected the *sachems*, or chiefs, and if a *sachem* proved unsuitable, they could depose him. Men selected the war chiefs, but the women could veto a war chief's decisions. When an Iroquois Matron spoke, people had to listen.

As a young woman being groomed to be a Matron, Molly was likely introduced to all of the leading white people of the region. That was probably how she met the outgoing Irishman William Johnson, one of the most important men in the colony. Johnson became the focus of Molly Brant's life, and had a profound influence on the career of her brother, Joseph.

A highly successful trader, soldier, and administrator, Johnson had acquired vast tracts of land in the Mohawk Valley. A community built on his land was called Johnstown after him. He was even knighted for his efforts against the French in the Seven Years War (in which the British captured Canada). Sir William ruled his private realm like a kindly king. He was a sociable man, friend to white and Native alike – at a time when most British officials regarded Native people as inferior. Because of his good relationship with the Six Nations, he was made Superintendent of Indian Affairs for the colony of New York. By all accounts Sir William was instantly attracted to Molly Brant by her beauty. Later in life she would, unfortunately, be scarred by smallpox. But that would make no difference to Johnson. Molly's looks first drew him to her, but it was her spirit and intelligence that held him there.

Sir William and Molly were married in a Native ceremony in 1759. She was about 23; he was 44. Not being wed according to British law was a wise move for both of them. If Molly had married Johnson according to white law and taken his name, she would have lost her status as a Mohawk Matron. By remaining Molly Brant, she not only maintained her position, but increased Sir William's already high regard among the Mohawk – especially after she bore him their first son, Peter. The Iroquois found Sir William to be loyal and honest, qualities which they greatly admired and found sadly lacking in many of the other whites. Johnson's lifelong efforts to have the Natives treated fairly earned him the honorary title of *sachem*, and the name *Warraghiyagey* (Doer of Great Things). The Mohawk would later say of him, "Sir William never deceived us."

Molly moved into Fort Johnson, Sir William's mansion on the Mohawk River. This was a large house surrounded by a cluster of smaller buildings where Johnson's servants, slaves, and an assortment of craftsmen and their families lived and worked. Families of Dutch, German, Irish, Scottish, and English origin lived on tenant farms in the surrounding countryside. Fort Johnson was very much like a feudal manor house. Dignitaries from both the white and Native communities came to pay their respects and do business. Molly was in charge of what was, in effect, a family company. She had to oversee the provisioning of the estate, which meant that she had to be able to read and write. It's possible that she learned this at the same school in which Sir William had enrolled her brother. He had taken young Joseph's development to heart.

In Sir William's absence Molly had to be hostess to the many people, white and Native, upper class and common, who came to Fort Johnson. She had to do it all with efficiency, and with the dignity of a woman who was both the lady of the house and a Matron of the Wolf Clan of the Mohawk Nation.

Fitting well into two worlds was not easy. Molly spoke fluent English, but preferred to converse in Mohawk. She wore Native-style clothes, but they were made from European material. Johnson had a family physician, but Molly was an expert in the use of herbs and other natural medications. She had to win over Sir William's other children, some of whom were almost as old as she was, while caring for her own mixed-blood sons and daughters.

In 1762 Molly's responsibilities increased when Sir William built the stately Johnson Hall on the Mohawk River. This mansion was even larger than Fort Johnson, to accommodate the unending parade of visitors. One guest reported seeing "sixty or eighty" Natives there at one time. They came not only to talk to Sir William, but also because of Molly's legendary generosity. They always went away with presents of food, clothing, and other goods. There was diplomacy in this, as gift-giving was important in

Iroquois culture. Molly's distribution of presents greatly enhanced her prestige as a Matron. So did her presence at the many negotiations that took place at Johnson Hall.

Molly's brother was a frequent visitor. Sir William took Joseph under his wing, educated him, and instructed him in the ways of white society. Even before Molly and Johnson were wed, Joseph participated in Sir William's actions against the French. Joseph would go on to become one of the most renowned Native leaders in North American history. The fatherly attention given him by his white brother-in-law helped prepare him for the outstanding role he would one day assume.

No sooner was Johnson Hall completed than trouble flared up on the Western frontier. Sir William flanked his mansion with two stone block-houses for protection. The unbelievably bad policies of the British governor, Sir Jeffrey Amherst, had so angered the Natives that by 1763 they were boiling for war. Amherst had absolutely no understanding of Natives, and stubbornly refused to listen to men like Sir William Johnson, who did understand them. Amherst placed harsh restrictions on trade and refused to acknowledge the tribes as masters in their own lands. It was even whispered that he authorized the sale of smallpox-infected blankets to the unsuspecting Natives.

Several of the tribes rose in fury under the leadership of the Ottawa chief Pontiac, and swept down on frontier homesteads and undermanned forts. Before the fighting could be stopped, more than 2,000 people were slain. The Senecas had joined Pontiac's war, and it was largely through the efforts of Sir William and Molly that the rest of the Iroquois Confederacy were kept from joining, too. When the hostile Natives and the British finally agreed to meet to come to terms, some of the meetings were held at Johnson Hall. In December 1764, more than 900 Natives were camped around Johnson's mansion. Molly's presence was important, not only because she was a Matron but because she could interpret. Good interpreters were scarce, and a single word incorrectly translated could result in potentially dangerous misunderstandings.

The British promised to stop moving white settlers onto Native lands, and established a line the colonists were forbidden to cross. The American settlers and greedy land speculators resented this. First hundreds, then thousands of settlers poured across the line. Inevitably there were bloody clashes between the frontiersmen and the Natives. A worried Sir William exhausted himself trying to keep the peace.

On July 11, 1774, in the midst of a great conference with the Six Nations at Johnson Hall, Sir William died at the age of 59. The Iroquois mourned the loss of their friend, and none more than Molly Brant. Even years later, she could not speak his name without weeping. After Sir William's death, his son Sir John Johnson took possession of Johnson Hall, and Molly moved back to her old home at Fort Johnson. She was not there long before the rebellion became war.

By this time the forests and farmlands in the northern part of the colony of New York were ablaze with the fires of revolution. Communties and even families were divided over the issue of independence from Great Britain. About a third of the population had joined the rebels, who wanted independence, and were calling themselves Patriots. Another third had decided to remain loyal to King George III of England, and called themselves Loyalists. The rest of the people wanted to stay neutral and keep out of the conflict altogether.

The American Revolution was, in fact, a civil war between English-speaking peoples. The Six Nations of the Iroquois Confederacy, who occupied the Mohawk Valley and land among the southern shore of Lake Ontario, wanted to stay out of it — at least at the beginning of the war — but that was almost impossible. The battlefields were all around them, and both sides wanted them as allies. Joseph Brant knew that the American Patriots wanted Native lands. He believed that his people's best hope lay with the British. The British had promised that once the rebellion was crushed, the Natives would keep their own territories. Brant gradually convinced most of the Iroquois to fight for the king. However, the Oneida and some of the Tuscarora fought for the Patriots, believing that the Americans would allow them to keep their land. They were wrong. The old Iroquois Confederacy was broken.

For their part, the British were well aware of the advantage of having Molly Brant on their side. When the Seneca began to waver in their support of the British, Molly took on one of their chiefs in public debate. She warned him, and all who were listening, that the Americans wanted their land, and reminded them that they had promised their loyalty to the king. She spoke with all the eloquence she could summon. By the time Molly was finished, the Seneca had resolved to continue their alliance with the British.

Most of the Natives, including Molly, were forced out of their homes, and the beautiful Mohawk Valley was devastated by war. The Natives, along with thousands of white Loyalist refugees, fled to British strongholds along the Canadian frontier. Molly went to Niagara, living on credit because she had lost almost everything. She and the rest of her people expected to return to their old homes when the war was over. She could not know that the people, white and Native, gathered under the protection of Fort Niagara and other British posts, would one day be the nucleus of a new place called Upper Canada.

Molly sent her daughters to Montréal to attend school, and spent much of her time visiting the tribes ". . . encouraging them to preserve their Fidelity." After visiting her daughters in Montréal, Molly went to the British base on Carlton Island in the St. Lawrence, where many Native refugees had sought shelter. The commander there, Captain Alexander Fraser, reported that the good behavior of the Natives ". . . is in great measure to be ascribed to Miss Molly Brant's influence, which is far superior to that of all their chiefs put together." Molly was also engaged in some espionage, getting information on rebel activity.

Eventually, the Americans were able to turn the tide of the war. In October 1781, Britain's Lord Cornwallis surrendered his army to the Americans and the French at Yorkton, bringing an end to the conflict. Britain's Native allies were excluded from the peace negotiations and no provision was made for them in the treaty signed by the United States and Great Britain in 1782. In that treaty, Britain signed away Native lands it did not even own.

Shocked by this betrayal, the Natives, led by Molly's brother, demanded that the British compensate them for their lost lands. Thousands of white Loyalists, driven from their homes by the victorious Americans, were being resettled in Canada. What about the Natives? The British negotiated with the Mississauga tribe of what is now Southern Ontario, and purchased land in the Grand River Valley as a new home for the Mohawks and any others of the Six Nations who wanted to go there. A community established there became the city of Brantford.

Molly visited the Six Nations Reserve, but she never made her home there. All but one of her daughters were now married, and Molly had become a grandmother. Molly went to live in Kingston, near one of her daughters, with a house and a pension provided by the government. She became a leading member of the community, and continued to be a voice in Native Councils.

The British surrender did not end Native warfare. Natives living on what the Americans now considered their land continued to resist white settlement. The American government, aware of Molly's high status among the Natives, offered her a large sum of money if she would return to the United States. Molly considered it a bribe to lure her into speaking to the hostile tribes on behalf of the United States. She turned it down.

Now approaching the age of 60, Molly was tired and no longer active in political affairs. She was interested only in her family. It stung when some of her own people criticized her and her brother for being too friendly with the British, and questioned their "Indian-ness." She felt that she and Joseph had always had their people's best interests at heart, and had done all they could in very trying times. The Brants always maintained that for Natives forced to choose between the British and the Americans, the British were the lesser of the two evils.

Molly Brant died on April 16, 1796, at her daughter's Kingston home. Her funeral was attended by members of the government, British officers, and leaders of the Iroquois community. The Mohawk Matron who had been driven from her home by the Americans would be remembered in Canada as a heroine – a woman who had dared to make her voice heard in two worlds.

4

Dr. James Miranda Barry

Barrier-breaker

The bright red sleigh careened at top speed through the quiet snowy streets of Montréal, Canada East, in the winter of 1858. Cursing "in a voice like the squall of an angry seagull," one of the city's most distinguished citizens yelled at his driver and footman whenever they hit an icy rut. He was dressed in the most elaborate uniform and sported a sword that was much too long for his small frame. Indeed, there was much that was unusual about Dr. James Miranda Barry. The people of Montréal did not know quite what to make of him.

In his mid-60s (elderly for that time), the army surgeon had been sent from England to Canada the previous year to be Inspector-General of barracks and hospitals. In more than 40 years of service with the British army in various outposts of the Empire, Dr. Barry had become one of the most well-known medical men of his time. Though not of aristocratic birth, he had earned the right to call himself "gentleman." He rubbed shoulders with nobility, and was invited to the finest homes wherever he went. In Montréal he was a founding member of the upper-class St. James Club.

The doctor stood barely 5 feet (1.5 meters) tall and was as smooth-cheeked as a schoolboy, though no one had ever seen him shave. No one, in fact, had ever seen him change his clothes or bathe. The doctor seemed extraordinarily modest for a medical man, and always went to great lengths to ensure that he had private quarters wherever he was stationed or when traveling by ship. When he was sick, Dr. Barry would not allow other doctors to give him a thorough examination. He even gave orders that there was to be no post-mortem done on his body when he died.

Unlike most other military men of the time, he drank very little alcohol. He was a vegetarian. He was insubordinate to his superiors. Charming and flirtatious with the ladies, he was short-tempered and acid-tongued in male company. According to one colleague, Dr. Barry lacked "all the outward signs of manly virility." Nonetheless, he could swear like a drill sergeant, and on several occasions had challenged men to duels over things most other gentlemen would have considered trivial.

Dr. Barry admitted to having "peculiar habits," and even the English writer Charles Dickens, who certainly was familiar with odd characters, said that the doctor was "unique in appearance and eccentric in manner." No one knew anything about the doctor's boyhood. He seemed just to have appeared on Earth at about the age of 15. But there was a reason, a good one, for all the mystery and contradictions surrounding this brilliant surgeon who helped to revolutionize 19th-century medicine. Dr. James Miranda Barry was a woman, in an age when both the medical profession and the British army were strictly male territory.

"James Miranda Barry" came into the world somewhere in the British Isles about 1795. Biographers believe that "James" was actually Margaret Bulkley, eldest daughter of Mary Anne and Jeremiah Bulkley of Ireland. Marriage problems and financial difficulties forced Mary Anne and young Margaret to go to London to seek assistance from Mary Anne's brother, James Barry, who was a famous artist. The painter turned his sister away, but helped his niece with some financial security. In an indirect way, he was also instrumental in the dramatic change Margaret was about to make in her life.

Margaret wanted to study medicine, but that science was barred to women. The dissection and operating rooms were not places for "fair ladies." Margaret was not about to let anything stop her. She vanished at about the age of 15. In a strange coincidence, James Barry appeared – the "nephew" of the late, great artist.

Not only did Margaret adopt her uncle's famous name, she also came under the influence of some of his closest friends – men with revolutionary ideas for their time. Lord Buchan, who became young James Barry's patron, was an outspoken advocate of education for females. Francisco Miranda, from whom James borrowed his second name, would eventually become a revolutionary hero in South America. Dr. Edward Fryer was one of the leading physicians of his time, and a pioneer of new medical ideas.

In the early 19th century, medical schools in England were closed to Roman Catholics like James, so in 1809 he went off to Scotland to enroll in the University of Edinburgh. Young James Miranda Barry wanted to be more than a physician, however. He wanted to be a surgeon.

Modern surgery was still in its infancy, and people regarded surgeons with awe and suspicion. Many simply did not trust men who cut into human bodies, living or dead. To ordinary people it was a gruesome practice and went against their religious beliefs. Laws made it difficult for medical schools to obtain bodies for dissection. Only the corpses of executed murderers could be legally used for anatomy classes. Medical schools had to resort to buying bodies from grave robbers – criminals who were ghoulishly dubbed "resurrection men." Dissection rooms were unsanitary and foul smelling. Teachers and students often became ill from close contact with diseased bodies. Dissection was also seen as a form of entertainment. Tickets were sold to the public, and the doctor doing the dissection had to be as much performer as surgeon.

Edinburgh was a fortunate choice for James Barry. A new breed of doctors was teaching medicine with a new scientific approach, making the university one of the best medical schools in Britain. James was also happy to find doctors at Edinburgh who were advancing knowledge in a field in which he was keenly interested – the female body.

Previously, doctors had dismissed women's medical problems, particularly pregnancy and childbirth, as unimportant. At Edinburgh, Barry was able to study both midwifery and gynecology. In time he would become a renowned authority on the treatment of venereal diseases, and would be the first British surgeon to successfully perform a cesarean section.

University students at the time were a riotous bunch. They played pranks, held wild drunken parties, and caroused in the streets. James Barry, however, was a quiet student who devoted all of his time to his studies. He lived under the guardianship of his "aunt" Mary Anne Bulkley. His sharp tongue and short temper kept fellow students from becoming too friendly with him. Barry's rudeness was probably meant to keep the young men at a distance so that no one would discover his secret. One student became a friend and tried to teach him boxing, but gave it up when James kept folding his arms across his chest to protect it from blows. Barry loved fine clothes and always dressed in the "dandy" fashion of the day – maybe because the padded jackets, pantaloons, and stockings were designed to make a slim figure appear more masculine.

James Miranda Barry graduated from the University of Edinburgh. With his diploma of Doctor of Medicine in hand, he was now free to go to London to continue his surgical studies. His late uncle's connections opened doors for him, but although he could have practiced in London's desirable social circles, he made a startling decision in 1813. He joined the British army as a regimental surgeon.

There could have been many reasons for his becoming an army doctor. It meant a regular payday – important for a youth with no family fortune to fall back on. It almost certainly meant service in the colonies, where as a doctor he would enjoy an officer's rank and would have private quarters. But there was quite likely another reason. Thanks to his uncle's friends and some of the visionary doctors he had studied under in Edinburgh, James Barry had developed a strong social conscience. He cared about the people who were often neglected by the medical institutions of the time: women, poor people, prostitutes, and the mentally ill. As an army surgeon, James Barry would care for the common soldiers.

The redcoat troops who manned the outposts of the British Empire were treated just as poorly as women when it came to medical care. Officers, who generally came from the privileged upper classes, received the best the army had to offer – good food, comfortable lodging, personal servants, a lively social life, and the finest medical care available. Not so for the rank-and-file foot soldiers. These men were mainly from the poverty-stricken slums of the cities or poor rural areas. The army cared little for their comfort and health. Soldiers lived in cramped, unsanitary barracks; their diet was poor and monotonous. Depending on where a soldier was posted, his drinking water might come from a sparkling river or a disease-ridden swamp. A British soldier could be sent to Jamaica, where he was exposed to strange tropical diseases, or to Canada, where he was unprepared for the cold. He was expected to march, drill, and fight in any kind of weather. If he dared to complain, he could end up at the whipping post.

It was a fact of army life that more soldiers died of sickness than of wounds inflicted on the battlefield. Even in peacetime, army hospitals were always full. For those who *were* wounded in battle, the army hospital was hell on earth. Anesthetics were unknown and amputation was the most common treatment. Surgeons got their nickname of 'sawbones' because they usually just sawed off injured arms and legs. There were no antibiotics, so infections ran wild. For many a soldier, the only escape from the hardships of army life was through alcohol, which often led to other problems.

While some army doctors were good, dedicated men, others were in the service because they were alcoholic or were too incompetent to run a successful private practice. As far as the military high command was concerned, the common soldier deserved no better. A soldier was supposed to be tough. If he died, there were plenty more where he came from. Dr. James Miranda Barry – formerly Margaret Bulkley – would spend the rest of his life fighting that inhumane attitude.

In 1816 Barry was sent to the Cape Colony at the southern tip of Africa. It was the beginning of a career that would take him on long tours of duty through some of Britain's most isolated outposts. Margaret Bulkley, disguised as a man, would make her mark in South Africa, Mauritius, Jamaica, Trinidad, Malta, Corfu, and Canada, with only brief stays in England. While treating soldiers, civilians, slaves, lepers – *anyone* who needed his help – Barry became an expert on tropical diseases. He was not afraid to put himself at risk while caring for others, and several times he fell dangerously ill. He spoke out against slavery, which was finally outlawed in the British Empire in 1834, and won the praise of the Duke of Wellington, Britain's most celebrated general.

In 1821 Barry was sent to the island of St. Helena to tend to the exiled French emperor, Napoleon Bonaparte. Bonaparte died, however, before Dr. Barry arrived. In 1855 Barry visited Florence Nightingale's hospital in Istanbul and had the nerve to scold the legendary nurse in public for not properly protecting herself from the heat of the sun. Miss Nightingale, who was a giant herself in the pioneering days of medicine, did not appreciate the little doctor's humiliating lecture. In a letter to her sister, she claimed that Barry "behaved like a brute" and called him "the most hardened creature I ever met."

More than anyone, Dr. Barry cared about the much-abused common soldier. He tried to convince commanding officers that much of the illness that killed the soldiers could be *prevented* through simple common sense. To Barry, it seemed obvious. Give the men clean water and a healthy diet. Don't drill them in extreme heat or cold. Dispose of garbage and human waste properly. Construct dry, clean, well-ventilated barracks. Make sure the soldiers keep themselves, their clothing, and their bedding clean. Barry also waged a one-man war against the quack doctors and peddlers of fake medicines who preyed on superstitious, uneducated soldiers. He reported corrupt officers who lined their own pockets with money that should have been used for the purchase of food, medical supplies, and the upkeep of hospitals.

When officers refused to go along with his recommendations, Barry sent strongly worded letters to England. One contemporary described these letters as "icy blasts down the staid corridors of the Colonial Secretary's office." Needless to say, Barry made enemies, and on one occasion was sent back to England under arrest.

When he heard of his new appointment to Canada, Barry commented, "So I am to go to Canada to cool myself after such a long residence in the Tropics and *Hot* Countries." He was in the country just under two years. Barry was based in Montréal, but was responsible for barracks and hospitals in Québec City, Toronto, and Kingston as well. A quick tour revealed the same old problems he'd found in other British colonies. The soldiers were fed an unchanging daily ration of one pound of boiled beef and one pound of bread. Barry immediately called for a change of diet and for ovens to be installed in barracks kitchens so that soldiers could have "the cheering change of a roast instead of eternal boiled beef and soup." When the lieutenant-general in command ignored this suggestion, Barry subjected him to an avalanche of letters until he agreed.

Then Barry turned his attention to the open sewers that ran through the military compound at Québec City. Once the sewers were taken care of, he targeted the bedding provided for the troops. The soldiers' mattresses and pillows, as well as those in the army hospitals, were stuffed with straw – the cheapest material available. Barry demanded that the straw be replaced with hair or feathers, ". . . as it must be evident the great comfort it would be to a poor sufferer to rest his emaciated and feverish limbs on something more genial than hard straw."

Throughout his career Dr. Barry also had campaigned against a problem that was chronic with armies everywhere – drunkenness among the soldiers. In Canada, he took aim at what he thought was the main reason that the soldiers drank too much: the failure of the army to provide private accommodation for married soldiers and their wives. The soldiers' wives lived in barracks rooms with 10 or 20 men. Barry felt this humiliated the women and drove them – and their husbands – to drink. Barry argued that the married soldiers and their wives should have rooms where they could have some privacy, ". . . that they might live with decency and bring up their children in the fear of God, without being tainted with the awful and disgusting language of a barracks room."

Dr. Barry won this fight and considered it a great personal victory. But the hard-won victory came at a price. Barry's age, the Canadian climate, and the strain of constant bickering with stubborn officers wore him down. Late in 1858 he suffered a severe attack of bronchitis. By spring he was too weak even to visit his beloved St. James Club. In May of 1859 he returned to England. He was ordered to appear before a medical board in London. It broke his heart when the board declared him unfit for further service, and retired him. He begged to be sent back to Canada, but his request was denied.

Except for a brief trip to Jamaica, Dr. Barry spent his last years in London, living in a house on – ironically – Margaret Street. In the summer of 1865 an epidemic of chronic diarrhea swept through the city, killing hundreds of people. The sickness was caused by one of Dr. Barry's old enemies, tainted water resulting from poor sanitation. James Miranda Barry, once Margaret Bulkley, died of the disease on July 25.

For more than 50 years Margaret had kept her secret. Once, in Trinidad, while Barry was bedridden with illness, another doctor and an officer had pulled back the sheet covering the unconscious patient. To their amazement they saw that the naked body under the sheet was not male, but female. When Barry awoke and learned of their discovery, he swore the two men to secrecy. They must have kept their promise. But now, in death, the secret was about to be revealed. A servant named Sophia Bishop was given the task of preparing the doctor's body for burial. It was she who discovered that Dr. James Barry was, as she put it, "a perfect female."

No post-mortem was performed on Dr. Barry's remains, and after the burial the medical and military men tried to keep Sophia Bishop hushed up. But the story gradually leaked out and spread. Some people who had known Barry well expressed shock and said that they had never suspected for a moment that the doctor was really a woman. Others claimed to have wondered all along, but said they had chosen to remain silent. Still others called Sophia Bishop a liar.

The debate over Dr. Barry's sex continues to this day. There is some suggestion that the doctor was a hermaphrodite, a person of mixed gender. That can never be proven. What is certain is that Mary Anne Bulkley had a baby whom she had baptized as Margaret, and that Margaret lived up to her middle teens as a girl. Margaret disappeared without a trace shortly before James came on the scene as the 'nephew' of Mary Anne and her brother. Handwriting in a letter composed by Margaret is identical to that of documents written by Dr. James Barry. All of the evidence indicates that a brave young woman secretly dared to invade the all-male worlds of medicine and the military, and in so doing helped to make the world a better place.

5

Mary Ann Shadd

Freedom Fighter

The boy made it! He had escaped from his master in the South, traveled the Underground Railroad, and crossed the border into Canada. He had no shoes, hat, or coat, but he was free! He had made it to the town of Chatham, Canada West (Ontario), where so many other black people had settled. The slave-catchers who had chased him all the way to the border couldn't touch him here. Slavery was illegal in Canada, and the hated Fugitive Slave Act could not reach across the border. *Or could it?*

Suddenly, the terrified boy found himself surrounded by several grim-looking white men – white men who spoke with Southern accents! They grabbed him and told him he was going back; back to his master where he belonged. The boy struggled, but the men were too strong for him. Then another pair of hands seized him. Black hands. A black woman's hands!

The woman who had rushed to the rescue tore the boy from the grasp of the slave-catchers. Before the bewildered white men knew what was happening, she hauled the frightened boy to the town courthouse and began to ring the bell. She rang it so violently that within moments a crowd of people, black and white, had formed on the street. The angry mob rushed at the slave-catchers, who turned on their heels and fled for their lives. The boy who had traveled from the American South using the

Underground Railroad was indeed now safe in Canada. His rescuer was
Mary Ann Shadd.

The Underground Railroad, of course, was not a railroad at all, but a
series of secret routes traveled by black people fleeing from slavery in the
American South. Heroic people all along the routes risked their lives to
guide runaways north to freedom in Canada. But what happened to the
freedom-seekers once they stepped onto Canadian soil? Were they welcomed by white Canadians? Now that they had escaped from physical
slavery, who would help them free their minds from the fear, ignorance,
and superstitions that were the baggage of that evil institution? Mary Ann
Shadd was willing to take on that task.

Mary Ann Camberton Shadd was actually born in the United States, in
Wilmington, Delaware, in 1823. She was the eldest of the 13 children of
Abraham and Harriett Shadd. Delaware was a slave state, but the Shadds
were Free Blacks. Nonetheless, young Mary grew up in a society domi-
nated by slavery. She knew its evils and she experienced the humiliation of
racial prejudice. She learned early in life to despise slavery and intolerance.
Her parents were active in the movement to abolish slavery, and their
house was a station on the Underground Railroad. Giving assistance to
runaway slaves was extremely dangerous. It could mean a prison sentence
if a person were caught at it. Even worse, in Delaware and other Southern
states it could even mean death at the hands of a proslavery lynch mob.

In the American South of the mid-1800s, blacks and whites alike were
taught from the cradle that blacks were an inferior race, fit only for work.
White Southerners believed they had a right to own slaves. They quoted
biblical passages and so-called "scientific facts" that they said proved their
arguments. They hated the outsiders for upsetting what they considered
their traditional way of life. Even though people in the Free states of the
North and in Canada were against slavery, many of them still believed that
blacks could never be equal with whites. Some wanted to free the slaves,
and then send them "home" to Africa.

The Shadd family certainly did not agree with this. Mary's father firmly believed that with education and fair opportunities, blacks could take their place in society and live together with whites. He passed on his beliefs to Mary.

Mary Shadd had an advantage that slave children didn't have. She attended school. In the South it was against the law to teach slaves to read and write. Mary was disgusted by this, so after she graduated, at age 16, she opened a school for black students in Wilmington. In addition to teaching, Mary wrote articles for a newspaper called the *North Star*. It was devoted to the abolition of slavery. Her writings and her work as a teacher caught the attention of Frederick Douglass, a former slave who was one of the most active black abolitionists in America.

Before 1850, the Free states of the North were safe for escaped slaves. But under pressure from the South, the American government passed the Fugitive Slave Act. This law allowed slave-owners, or their paid "slave-catchers," to chase runaways into the northern states, catch them, and return them to the South. This law also ordered northern law officers to help the slave-catchers whether they wanted to or not. It even allowed slave-catchers to seize Free Blacks. All the slave-catcher needed was for one white person in the South to claim that the captive was a runaway.

The black population of the North, both Free Blacks and escaped slaves, started looking at Canada as the place where they could be safe. One of those who decided to move north to Canada was Mary Ann Shadd.

Mary arrived in Canada West in September of 1851. The British colony was already a haven for black Americans. In the 1790s the first governor of Upper Canada, John Graves Simcoe, had outlawed slavery, and in 1834 it had been abolished throughout the British Empire. Canada's role in providing refuge for runaway slaves had made southern slaveholders furious. They referred to Canada as "the vile, sensuous, animal, infidel, superstitious Democracy of Canada." They tried to scare their slaves by spreading exaggerated tales about the cold Canadian climate, ravenous wild animals, and

Indian raids. They told their slaves that Canada was thousands and thousands of miles away and that the rivers separating the U.S. from Canada were raging torrents, many miles wide.

One slave who didn't buy these false stories was Henry Bibb of Kentucky. He escaped to Canada, settling at Sandwich, near Windsor. There he published a newspaper called *The Voice of the Fugitive*, while his wife, Mary, taught school. Bibb's publication was of great importance because it served Canada West's growing black community. Many (but not all) of his readers had been slaves. Bibb also was Secretary of the Fugitives Union Association and a founding member of the Refugee Home Society. He was one of the most important and influential black men in Canada. Ironically, Henry and Mary Bibb were about to become bitter foes of Mary Ann Shadd.

When Mary Shadd left Delaware, she went first to Toronto. She wrote to one of her brothers, ". . . I have been here more than a week, and like Canada. Do not feel prejudice and repeat if you were to come here . . . you would do well . . . [every] man is respected and patronized [according] to his ability. . . ." Soon after her arrival in 1851, she met Henry and Mary Bibb at an antislavery meeting. At the meeting she learned that teachers were needed in the Windsor area. Windsor was one of the main crossing points for fugitive slaves, and had a large black community. Unfortunately, black children were not welcome in white schools, nor was there a place for adult blacks who wanted to learn to read and write.

Mary Shadd set up her school in an abandoned army building called the Old Barracks, which dated back to the War of 1812. It was a drafty old building in bad shape that also was used to shelter newly arrived fugitives. Mary had about a dozen children in her day school and 11 adults for night classes. Aside from the building itself, which was almost impossible to heat in cold weather, Mary had two major problems – money and the Bibbs.

In those days, a teacher's pay was exceedingly low, and for Mary the situation was even worse. She began by charging students 50 cents a month, but when she found that most families couldn't afford that, she lowered her fee to 37 cents. Even then, few families could spare the money. Some parents tried to pay for the school with firewood instead of cash, but after a while the fuel donations stopped, too.

As well as her own living expenses, Mary had to pay for school supplies out of her own pocket. The Bibbs suggested that she ask the American Missionary Association (AMA) headquarters in New York City for help. Mary asked the AMA for $250 a month – the average salary for a teacher. The AMA agreed to only $125. It was not enough. Mary decided that, for the time being, she would not tell the parents of her students that she was getting help from a charity. She thought if the parents knew this, they might feel they didn't have to pay the tuition fees. Mary intended to tell them at a later date, when she was better established. This "secret" would cause her a lot of trouble later.

Meanwhile, Mary had to find a way to earn more money. She wrote a booklet entitled *Notes of Canada West*. It was a collection of facts about Canada that would be useful to black Americans who were considering coming to the country. Mary's booklet provided truthful information on Canada's climate, geography, and government, as well as pointers on farming and employment. It told readers that in Canada, if they obeyed the law and took the oath of allegiance, they would "enjoy full privileges of British birth in the Province." In fact, it *encouraged* them to choose Canada. But in the U.S. black leaders such as Frederick Douglass were against emigration.

Mary Shadd did not believe in all-black communities, schools, and churches. She argued for integration. Only by living together, she claimed, could blacks and whites come to know and understand each other and overcome their fears and suspicions. She had no patience with prejudice between the two races, whether, came from blacks or whites.

Henry Bibb strongly disagreed with Mary. He believed in segregation and thought that black people needed their own communities, schools, and churches. To promote his plan, he and a white missionary, Reverend Charles C. Foote, had founded the Refugee Home Society (RHS). This organization purchased land and resold it under specific conditions to runaway slaves who had made it to Canada. Mary felt from the start that the RHS was going about things the wrong way, however good its intentions. In time, she even came to doubt those "good intentions."

Because he disagreed with her, Bibb would not publish Mary's booklet on Canada West, so she had it printed in Detroit. When Bibb reviewed it in his newspaper, he both praised and criticized the booklet. Mary was upset at this. She had been having difficulties at school, too. She observed that Henry Bibb, who sometimes taught bible classes, was not qualified to do so. She also disliked Mrs. Bibb's teaching methods. She considered Mrs. Bibb to be harsh and suspected her of being "a drug-taking woman."

In June 1852, Henry Bibb revealed in his newspaper the fact that Mary Ann Shadd had received money for her school from the AMA. This was devastating to Mary, because it made her appear to be dishonest. Bibb also claimed that Mary, who was for integration of blacks and whites, was running a segregated school for blacks only. This was not true, as Mary had opened her school to both black and white students.

Then Mary began to openly question the policies of the Refugee Home Society that Bibb and Rev. Foote had started. She asked why the organization reached out to fugitive blacks, but did nothing for Free Blacks coming to Canada. Many Free Blacks arrived just as poor and homeless as the former slaves. She pointed out that black people could purchase land from the government on much better terms than those offered by the Refugee Home Society. Moreover, they would have clear rights to the land, and would not be bound by the rules of the society, which she said served only Henry Bibb and his colleagues.

Bibb began to attack Mary Ann viciously in his newspaper. He said that her complaints added "nothing to her credit as a lady." Of course, Henry Bibb's articles hurt Mary, but what really bothered her was that they were being read by the very people she wanted to help – black people who were either already in Canada or thinking of coming. Henry Bibb was doing what many other editors of the time did. He was using his newspaper to express his own point of view, and he included large doses of falsehood. As Mary said in a letter to a friend, "What a vast amount of mischief a man like H. Bibb can do with [a newspaper] of his own to nod, insinuate, and 'fling' away the reputation of others . . ."

Mary thought about leaving the school, but eventually decided to stick with it, and "leave the result with God." But she could not let Henry Bibb's attacks on her character go without answer. She sent word around that she was holding a public meeting where she would address all of the statements made about her in the *Voice of the Fugitive*. When Henry Bibb learned of this he sent Mary a note, warning her that if she insisted on talking about these things at the meeting, it would be "the worst day's work" she ever did.

Mary held her meeting anyway, and one of the resolutions passed was that the work of Miss M. Shadd as a teacher was "highly appreciated." Bibb's newspaper, of course, gave the meeting only a brief mention.

That summer a cholera epidemic swept through the Windsor area. The Board of Health pronounced Mary's school unsafe, and when she reopened it in September only nine students showed up. Henry and Mary Bibb continued to make life miserable for her. She was attacked in almost every issue of their *Voice of the Fugitive*. The Bibbs also sent negative letters about her to the charitable foundation in New York that was supporting her. Finally, in January of 1853, she lost that financial support on "religious" grounds. Mary knew that religion had nothing to do with it. The real reason was her dispute with the Bibbs.

She continued to teach, difficult as that was with no money, but she was about to start another career that would have a far greater impact. Mary decided to fight fire with fire. She was going to publish her own newspaper, the *Provincial Freeman*. Mary Shadd was about to become the first black female editor and publisher in North America. But before Mary even started her new venture, she faced prejudice of a different nature. Readers would not accept a newspaper with a woman editor. There were a few female journalists at the time, writing mostly on topics such as fashion and social events. But for a woman to be writing about the important issues of the day or to edit a newspaper was simply unthinkable.

Luckily for her, she had a supporter. Samuel Ringgold Ward had visited Windsor the previous summer. A former slave, Ward was famous in the United Sates and Canada for his fight against slavery. He was an accomplished writer and a gifted speaker. At first Ward was impressed with Henry Bibb's newspaper and wrote some articles for him, but he soon came to share Mary Shadd's views on how the Refugee Home Society operated. Not surprisingly, he soon found himself being attacked in Henry Bibb's newspaper.

Ward agreed to lend his name to Mary's paper. Mary would do the editing and most of the writing, but the admired name of Samuel Ringgold Ward would appear as editor. Mary spent the next six months doing all the hard work that was necessary to bring a new publication into existence. At the same time, she continued to teach.

The schedule was exhausting enough. Then the preparations of the final weeks had to be rushed because of a tragedy. In the spring of 1853 Mary Shadd and Samuel Ward attended a meeting of a local debating society. Two of the young men at the meeting got into a fight outside and one of them was killed. In its report on the incident, Henry Bibb's paper blamed the people of Mary's upstart *Provincial Freeman*, accusing them of "holding illegal and uproarious meetings and thus encouraging violence." Of course, this was not true. But Mary had to rush the final preparations of her paper so she could publish an accurate account of the incident.

The first issue of her *Provincial Freeman* came out in March. Its front-page headline read: "Devoted to Anti-Slavery, Temperance, and General Literature." The publisher's motto was: "Self-Reliance is the True Road to Independence." Mary Shadd wanted to do more than just report the news. Her mission was to attack slavery and erase the stereotype of black people as childlike beings incapable of looking after themselves without white help. She believed Henry Bibb and his colleagues promoted this way of thinking.

One of her main targets was the practice of "begging" for money from black and white charities. Mary wrote that black people newly arrived in Canada needed a little help to get started in their new lives, but then they should make their own living. There were plenty of jobs available in the growing province, she said, and cheap land was available for farming. Mary pointed out that black people living on charity only reinforced the view that they were lazy and helpless. She also reported that much of the money donated by generous individuals and organizations went into the pockets of the people who collected it. She went so far as to say that Henry Bibb was one of those who profited at the expense of black immigrants.

Racism of any kind angered Mary Shadd. She advised refugees from the South to abandon any prejudices about white people that they might have brought with them from their slave days. She never claimed that prejudice did not exist in Canada, because it did. But in Canada, she pointed out, prejudice was not supported by law. A white person who committed an offence against a black person could be taken to court. British law did not discriminate, she told her readers.

Mary wrote about other things that concerned her as well. She was a strong advocate for women's rights. It must have frustrated her that she had to speak out for women from behind Samuel Ward's name, especially since, after the first issue of the paper was published, he had sailed for England.

As always, Mary fought on, and – as always – she had money problems. Newspapers needed subscribers in order to survive, and many publications had folded after one or two issues. After her first edition, Mary went on the road selling subscriptions for her *Provincial Freeman*. She traveled throughout the United States because that's where the biggest market was, and she wanted to convince black Americans that a better life awaited them in Canada. She attended meetings and gave lectures, even speaking in slave states. This was dangerous because the proslavery faction often resorted to violence.

Within a year, however, Mary had enough subscription support to resume her publication. She set up an office in Toronto and began distribution to all the centers of black population in Canada West, as well as in Nova Scotia and various American states. Mary's family moved up to Canada to help her. Her brother Isaac and sister Amelia wrote articles and sold subscriptions, but it was still difficult to make ends meet. Mary was particularly annoyed when Torontonians raised money for an American antislavery newspaper, the *North Star*, while ignoring the lively new paper that was being published right in their own city.

In October 1854, she took a risky step and revealed that she was the editor of the *Provincial Freeman*. The backlash against the very idea of a woman editor was so great that she was in danger of losing subscribers. Mary again had to have a man, this time a Reverend William P. Newman, "front" as the editor. She then explained to her readers that she only had taken the editor's position temporarily. Mary also moved the newspaper's headquarters to Chatham, where about a third of the population was made up of black immigrants.

Over the next few years the *Provincial Freeman* developed into what many historians consider the best abolitionist newspaper of the times. Even people like Frederick Douglass, who were not always in agreement with Mary Shadd, admired the paper. But getting it off the press and into the hands of readers was never easy. The lack of money sometimes meant the paper didn't appear on time. Besides writing articles and being "ghost" editor, Mary went on exhausting tours, trying to sell subscriptions. She and her sister also taught school in Chatham to help meet expenses. In spite of all its difficulties, though, the *Provincial Freeman* outlived Henry Bibb's *Voice of the Fugitive*, which ceased publication when Bibb died suddenly in 1854.

In 1856 Mary married Thomas Cary of Toronto, a widower with three children. Mary and Thomas had two children of their own, but Thomas died in 1860, just two months before the youngest was born. Two years earlier, Mary had met the controversial abolitionist John Brown when he visited Chatham. Brown wanted to end slavery by armed rebellion. In

October 1859, when Brown launched his doomed raid on Harper's Ferry, Virginia, a reporter named Osborne Anderson was with him. Anderson was from Mary's paper and he was the only member of Brown's group to escape death in battle or by execution. When he wrote a book about that historic event, Mary Shadd was the editor.

The American Civil War, which began in 1861, spelled the end of slavery in the United States, but only after four bloody years of fighting. Although Mary Ann Shadd had become a Canadian citizen in 1862, she went to the United States in 1864 to help recruit black soldiers for the Union army. She was the only woman officially listed by the U.S. government as a recruiter.

After the defeat of the South, with slavery finally abolished, many of the black people who had fled to Canada returned the U.S. Mary Shadd returned too, and taught school in Detroit. She was the first woman to enroll in Howard Law School, and although Mary completed her studies in 1872, she was not allowed to graduate until 1881. The school did not want to grant a diploma to a woman. Mary continued to write, to teach, and to fight tirelessly for human rights and against discrimination in all its forms.

Mary Ann Shadd died in Washington, D.C. on June 5, 1893. She had made enormous contributions to the hard fight against slavery. She had dared to enter the male-dominated world of the media and publish a newspaper. She had become one of the few female lawyers of the time. In her 70 years on the face of this Earth she made a mark that will never be erased.

6

Sarah Emma Edmonds

Nurse, Soldier, and Spy

It seems amazing that during the American Civil War (1861-1865), almost 400 women disguised themselves as men and joined the Union or Confederate Armies. But, in fact, this was not as difficult as it might seem. Medical examinations at enlistment posts were very simple. If a young man looked healthy, he was accepted. Many a smooth-faced lad, eager for excitement, lied about his age to sign up. Recruiting officers were desperate for bodies to fill the ranks and did not ask questions. So it was entirely possible for a young woman to pass herself off as a boy in his late teens. It is also a fact that thousands of Canadians marched with the armies of both the North and the South. One soldier in the Union (North) Army was both Canadian and a woman.

Sarah Emma Edmondson – she later shortened her name to Edmonds – was born in New Brunswick in 1841. She was the youngest of six children, five girls and one boy. Her father, Isaac, was a stern man who was disappointed that five of his children were girls, and that his only son was sickly. He drove his girls hard, expecting them to make up for the healthy sons he didn't have. When the girls weren't in school they were out in the fields, dressed like boys, doing the kind of work usually done by boys. To try to please her father, Sarah struggled hard to do well in things that were considered male activities – hunting, fishing, riding, and shooting.

Sarah grew up strong and tough. She was a crack shot and an expert rider, and even knew how to survive in the woods. But she never could win her father's approval. Isaac's harsh treatment of his wife and daughters gave young Sarah a very negative attitude toward men. "In our family the women were not sheltered, but enslaved," she later said in an interview. "Hence, I naturally grew up to think of man as the implacable foe of my sex."

Fortunately, Sarah's mother, Betsey, had a kind and loving nature. In the Edmondson household, as in most pioneer homes, the mother did the doctoring. Betsey was an excellent nurse. She knew how to make the home remedies and how to treat the injuries that came with rugged farm life. She passed on this knowledge, as well as a tender bedside manner, to her daughters.

Sarah was a tomboy who yearned for freedom. She got her first clue of how to achieve it when a traveling salesman gave her a book titled *Fanny Campbell, the Female Pirate Captain: a Tale of the Revolution*. It was a romantic story about a woman who found adventure by disguising herself as a man. That book, Sarah later said, was one of the greatest discoveries of her life. It was not long before she would try out the idea it had planted in her mind.

Meanwhile, while teenaged Sarah was dreaming of freedom, her father arranged a marriage for her — to a farmer many years older than she was. Sarah had no choice; there was no way she could refuse. But while wedding plans were being made, she ran away, apparently with the assistance of her mother. Sarah went to the town of Salisbury where she got a job in a ladies' hat shop. By 1858 she and a friend were running their own shop in Moncton. Then Sarah heard from her mother that her father had found out where she was and was coming for her. Sarah didn't waste any time. She cut her hair short, put on men's clothing, and fled to St. John. There she began a new life as 'Franklin Thompson.'

Frank Thompson soon landed a job selling bibles and other religious books in rural New Brunswick. The publisher, Hurlburt Publishing

Company, said they had never had a better salesman. Frank did so well that he could afford to dress like a fine gentleman and own a fashionable horse and buggy in which "he" took lady friends for rides. To make sure she wasn't discovered, Sarah even had a telltale mole removed from her cheek. When she paid a visit to her family – while Isaac was absent – her own mother and siblings didn't recognize her until she told them who she was.

Later, Sarah ran into bad luck, which she never explained, and lost all her money and her books, ". . . except for a Bible, my sample, and my valise." It was the dead of a snowy New Brunswick winter, but that wasn't enough to stop Sarah. She sold the bible for $5, and then set out for the headquarters of the Hurlburt Publishing Company in Hartford, Connecticut. Except for a few short rides she managed to get, she walked the entire 450 (725 km) miles!

She introduced herself to Mr. Hurlburt (who would later publish her autobiography) as Franklin Thompson, the young man who had been doing such a good job in New Brunswick. Hurlburt immediately made Frank the sales agent for Nova Scotia. Frank's 10-month stay in Nova Scotia was a complete success. He sold books, lived and traveled in style, and even proved to be a heartbreaker with the young ladies. No one suspected that the dashing young man was a girl – a girl who was not yet 20 years old.

By 1860 Sarah had decided that life must hold more exciting options for Frank Thompson than being a book salesman. So she went west to Flint, Michigan. As it happened, she was there on April 12, 1861, when the Civil War started in South Carolina. Five days later Frank Thompson enlisted as a nurse in the Flint Union Grays. Sarah later wrote that as a man she could help the sick and wounded men with "less embarrassment to them and to myself." She said she only wanted to ease the suffering. "I had inherited from my mother a rare gift of nursing, and when not too weary or exhausted, there was a magnetic power in my hands to soothe the delirium."

The Flint Union Grays became Company F of the 2nd Michigan Infantry. They went to Washington, D.C., where they were reviewed by President Abraham Lincoln. Everyone there thought that the war would be over in a few weeks and that the North's boys in blue would trounce the Southern rebel traitors without even working up a sweat. They had to think again after the First Battle of Bull Run on July 21, 1861. The rebel Confederate Army routed the North and sent the Yankees fleeing in panic back to Washington. Frank Thompson, who was treating wounded soldiers in a stone church, came within a hairsbreadth of being captured by the Confederates.

The Bull Run battle gave Sarah her first eye-opening experience of the horrors of war. Lead musket balls, iron cannon shot, and steel bayonets demolished human flesh and bone. Hospital conditions were primitive. There was no anesthetic and there were no antibiotics. Doctors dug bullets out of men with long steel probes. They amputated shattered limbs with an instrument that resembled a hacksaw. Surgeons waded in blood, and makeshift hospitals echoed with the screams of men in agony. In addition, the army camps were breeding grounds for epidemics. Sanitation was poor, the food and water were bad, and there was severe overcrowding. More soldiers fell to disease than fell on the battlefields. Through it all, Sarah struggled on. As Frank Thompson, she earned the reputation of being the kindest, most efficient, and most devoted male nurse in the regiment.

But Sarah was about to make an even more valuable and dramatic contribution. After the defeat at Bull Run, General George B. McClellan, a brilliant organizer, was put in charge of the army. He spent the next eight months training his army and organizing it into a fit fighting force. In addition to his nursing duties, Frank was told that he was also to be a mail courier.

This suited Sarah just fine. Couriers were constantly on the move, grabbing their sleep when and where they could, so Sarah would rarely have to sleep in a tent with other soldiers, where her secret might be discovered. As a courier Sarah also got to know the lay of the land very well. It might have been for this reason that Frank Thompson was summoned to General McClellan's headquarters. The general was looking for a spy to go behind enemy lines. Sarah was grilled on her political views and moral beliefs. She was also given a phrenological examination – doctors examined the shape of her head. It was believed that the shape of a person's head helped to determine character. Sarah passed easily, and not even the doctors suspected that 'Frank' was a woman.

General McClellan was preparing for a campaign against the rebels. But first he needed information on their defenses and the strength of their artillery. Frank Thompson volunteered to go. It was a brave decision because captured spies were not treated as prisoners of war. They were brutally questioned and then shot.

Sarah's first assignment was to infiltrate the Confederate defenses at Yorktown, Virginia. The Southern Army employed slaves for most of its manual work, so every rebel camp had a group of black people. Sarah disguised herself as a black man called Ned. She shaved her head and put on a wig of curly black hair. Then she blackened her head, face, neck, arms, hands, and dressed in the shabby clothing slaves wore. With a few crackers and a loaded pistol in her pocket, she slipped out of her own army camp at night, walked across country, and sneaked past the outermost Confederate lookouts.

She slept that night on the cold wet ground "in fear and trembling," as she wrote later. The next morning she entered Yorktown. There, a Confederate officer put 'Ned' to work with slaves who were building fortifications. She saw that some of the Confederate guns were actually only logs painted black and mounted on wheels so that from a distance they looked like cannons. By the end of the day Sarah's hands, unused to hard work, were raw and blistered. But in the evening no one questioned he wandered about the Confederate stronghold, making notes that ...ic hid in her shoe.

The next day 'Ned' was ordered to carry water to the soldiers. This gave Sarah the chance to eavesdrop and pick up more valuable information. She even saw the legendary Confederate general, Robert E. Lee.

Now Sarah had to get back to her Union lines. The chance came when 'Ned' was handed a rifle and ordered to go on lookout duty. A rebel sergeant told 'Ned' that if he fell asleep on watch, he'd be shot like a dog. The Confederates believed that the fear of punishment would keep the slaves from defecting to Union lines. That night, during a rainstorm, Sarah crept away from her post and entered the Union camp carrying a Confederate rifle as a prize.

Thanks partly to Sarah's information, General McClellan was able to force the rebels out of Yorktown and push on toward Williamsburg. There was heavy fighting there, and Frank Thompson was kept busy caring for the wounded from both sides. Among one group of injured rebel prisoners was the same sergeant who had threatened to shoot 'Ned' like a dog. He did not recognize the white Yankee nurse who was tending to him.

At Williamsburg, Frank Thompson again worked as a spy. This time Sarah disguised herself as a female Irish peddler. Thanks to her Irish mother, Sarah could speak in a convincing Irish accent. As 'Bridget' she crossed the Chickahominy River on horseback, then proceeded on foot toward the Southern lines. While sleeping in a swamp at night, however, she became seriously ill. She didn't know it at the time, but she had come down with malaria. For the next two days Sarah lay alone in hiding, consumed by fever. Then she wandered, sick, starving, and lost, until she came to a small white house in the woods. Inside she found a sick Confederate soldier. The man was the enemy, but Sarah did all she could for him. He told her his name was Allen Hall. He knew he was dying, and he gave her his gold watch and ring, and asked her to deliver them to a Major McKee in the Confederate camp. Sarah was sad to see yet another young man die, but she now had a good reason for going into the enemy camp.

Sarah searched the house and found some pepper, mustard, red ink, and ochre. Her own illness already had made her look very much like a refugee on the run from the Yankees. To make herself look even more convincing, she made a hot mustard mixture and blistered one side of her face. She rubbed some red ink around her eyes and used the ochre to darken her pale complexion. She put pepper into her handkerchief so she could make her eyes run with tears whenever she needed to "cry."

'Bridget' looked so sad and miserable that she had no trouble talking her way past the Confederate guards. Once inside the Southern camp, she kept her ears open. She soon learned of a trap the Confederates were planning to spring on the Union troops. She also found Major McKee, gave him the watch and ring Allen Hall had entrusted to her, and tearfully told him how the soldier had died. As it turned out, the soldier had been an officer and a close friend of Major McKee. The major wanted to give his comrade a decent Christian burial. He played right into Sarah's hand.

Major McKee gave 'Bridget' a horse, and told her to lead some of his soldiers back to the house in the woods so they could recover Hall's body. The house was dangerously close to Yankee territory, so while two soldiers went in to retrieve the corpse, the sergeant in command sent the others to stand watch. He told 'Bridget' to ride a little way down the road and warn him if she saw any Yankees. Of course, 'Bridget' did as she was told, and then some. Once the soldiers couldn't see her, she galloped her newly acquired rebel horse straight for the Union camp, where she described the enemy trap.

In the bloody battles that followed, Frank Thompson was made personal assistant to General Philip Kearny. Frank dashed around carrying messages and often came under fire. But Sarah believed God was protecting her, because not once was she hit. Her only war injury was a bite from her rebel horse.

On the eve of the 2nd Battle of Bull Run in August of 1862, Frank Thompson was again sent behind enemy lines. This time Sarah disguised herself as a female slave. In the rebel camp she was put to work cooking for the officers. Those men discussed battle plans as they ate, taking no notice of the black women who were cooking and waiting on them. In a matter of hours Sarah had the information she needed.

Then something unexpected happened. When she moved an officer's coat that had been draped over a stool, a bundle of papers fell out of the pocket. Sarah quickly snatched it up and hid it in her clothing. She slipped out of the rebel camp and made for the Union position, only to find herself in the middle of a battlefield. Sarah hid in the cellar of an old house, and was unhurt even when the cannon fire caused the building to collapse around her.

After the shooting died down, Sarah crawled out of the rubble and made it back to her own camp, where she handed over the bundle of papers. The documents turned out to be nothing less than details of the Confederate Army's plans for the capture of Washington, D.C.! The Union officers were so impressed with Frank Thompson's work that they sent Sarah on three more visits to the Confederate camp over the next 10 days. Each time she returned with vital information. The Union Army was able to keep the Confederates from advancing on Washington, but General Kearny was killed in the battle and General McClellan failed to pursue and destroy the rebel army.

President Lincoln replaced McClellan with General Ambrose Burnside. That incompetent officer sent his men to fight against a strongly fortified Confederate position in the Battle of Fredericksburg. It turned out to be the worst Union defeat of the whole war. Sarah was there to see the field piled with dead men, and literally running with blood. Lincoln immediately removed Burnside and sent him west to command the Union post in Kentucky. With Burnside went the 2nd Michigan Infantry – and Frank Thompson. Kentucky would be the scene of Sarah's last, and most dangerous, mission behind enemy lines.

Dressed in clothing taken from a rebel prisoner, Frank Thompson was sent to spy on enemy troop movements. At a farmhouse, Frank accidentally met a Confederate captain named Logan. This officer thought Frank was a young vagabond and immediately put him in the rebel army. The next day Sarah found herself on a horse with a Confederate cavalry unit, looking across a field at her own Union cavalry. There was every possibility that she would be shot by her own soldiers!

Captain Logan ordered the charge, and the rebel horsemen surged forward. Sarah held back, pretending that her horse was skittish. This trick allowed her to fall back from the hand-to-hand combat that broke out when the two lines clashed. In the confusion, she rode around to the Union side. One of her own officers recognized 'Frank,' and called out to her to fall in beside him. Before she could do that, Sarah suddenly found herself face to face with Captain Logan. She pulled out her pistol and shot him. Several other rebels now attacked her with their sabers, but the Union horsemen drove them off and saved her.

Frank Thompson's superiors now felt it was too dangerous to send him on further missions behind enemy lines. Instead, they put Frank to work as a detective, rooting out spies behind their own lines. Sarah's undercover work led to the arrest of three rebel spies in Louisville.

In the spring of 1863, Sarah fell ill with malaria again. Afraid that an army doctor would discover her secret, she slipped away from her regiment. She put on women's clothing, used the name Sarah Emma Edmonds, and went to a civilian doctor. As far as the army was concerned, Franklin Thompson had deserted.

When Sarah was well enough, she went to Pittsburg, Pennsylvania, where she wrote a book about her adventures titled *Nurse and Spy in the Union Army*. In the book she still hid the fact that she had been a woman posing as a man. The book became a bestseller. Sarah donated most of the profit to charities for wounded soldiers.

During the final months of the war, Sarah worked as a female nurse at army hospitals. She met a fellow New Brunswicker, Linus H. Seelye, and married him in 1867. Although the drama and adventure of years as a male soldier were over, Sarah was as dedicated as ever to doing good works. She and Linus helped raise and educate orphaned black children, and taught former slaves to read and write. Their own three children all died very young, so they adopted two boys.

Not until 1882 did Sarah finally reveal to the world that she had served in the Union Army as a man. She spoke up only because she wanted to establish a home for old soldiers and needed money to do it. She figured if she had a soldier's pension from the Army, her problem would be solved. It also had always bothered her that Frank Thompson had been listed as a deserter. She contacted the War Department in Washington, D.C., and told her whole story. For proof, she found as many of her old army comrades as she could. Needless to say, there were a lot of raised eyebrows and open mouths when veterans of the war learned that their old buddy Frank Thompson was a woman. There were a few who admitted that there had always been something "different" about Frank.

It took a long time, but Sarah finally managed to get the name of 'Franklin Thompson' stricken from the list of deserters, and in 1884 Sarah was granted an army pension. She did not receive any money, however, until five years later. In the end it was too small a sum to be of any use to her in building a home for old soldiers.

Oddly enough, Sarah and her family finally settled in Texas – a former Confederate state. She died on September 5, 1898. The inscription below her name on the gravestone simply reads: ARMY NURSE.

7

Pearl Hart

Ontario's Bandit Queen

The stagecoach robbery may be one of the most familiar images we have of the wild days of the Old West. The bandits draw their pistols, as the coach driver and the shotgun guard reach for the sky. Many of the most famous outlaws were stagecoach robbers and they were tough customers. But the last stagecoach hold-up in the dying days of the Old West was committed not by a dangerous bandit from Texas or Montana. It was pulled off by a woman – from Canada.

She was born about 1871 to a respectable middle-class family in Lindsay, Ontario. Not much is known of Pearl Taylor's early life, but there was no indication that she would ever set foot on the slippery slope to crime. She was described as attractive, witty, and outgoing. Perhaps she was *too* outgoing, for people said that she would go out with just about any young man who asked. Not exactly proper for a girl in Victorian Ontario.

At about the age of 17, Pearl was sent to a straightlaced boarding school in preparation for a good marriage to some upstanding young man. But the idea backfired. While Pearl was attending school, she met Frederick Hart. He was a personable and charming young man, and the teenaged Pearl fell head over heels in love with him. The couple eloped, and married.

For all his charm, however, Fred Hart was a wastrel, a rotten gambler, and a wife-beater. For a while the Harts traveled around Ontario, living in cheap rooming houses, while Fred tried to win at card tables and race-tracks. Occasionally he got jobs tending bar, but it was plain that knuckling down and working for a living did not agree with Fred Hart.

Pearl continued what she called her "nomadic life" with Hart, taking his abuse, until 1893, when they went to Chicago for the Columbian Exposition. Fred wanted to get in on some of the big time gambling that would be going on there, but the real cardsharps realized he was just a hustler and wouldn't let him in on the action. He had to settle for a job at as a barker at a sideshow, luring people in to see freaks and exotic dancing girls.

Pearl, meanwhile, wandered the fairgrounds and made the discovery that would change her life. A Wild West Show! She was enthralled by the cowboys, the Indian fighters, the sharpshooters, and the handsome, mascu-line frontiersmen who seemed to be everything her husband wasn't. She went back to the show again and again to watch the chases on horseback and the shoot'em-ups. Pearl was blinded by the romance of the West – a West that, in fact, had never really existed. Bidding good-bye to her no-good husband, she boarded a train for Trinidad, Colorado.

Pearl gave birth to a baby boy in Trinidad. According to an issue of the *Arizona Star*, "She wrestled with the world in a catch-as-catch-can style, making a living for herself and her baby son." With things not turning out as she had hoped, Pearl went home. She stayed only long enough to hand her infant son over to her mother.

She next turned up in Arizona, drifting from town to town, working as a cook, a laundress, and a maid. There wasn't much else available for a woman on her own. During this time, she learned to drink, smoke cigars, and swear like a trooper. In 1895 she ran into her husband in Phoenix. Hart poured out his woes to her. He said he was lost without her and must have her back. He even promised to get a job. That clinched it for Pearl. The idea of a secure home with a breadwinning husband was much more attractive than that of washing other people's laundry.

Fred did get a job, managing a hotel and tending bar, and Pearl had another child, a girl this time. For three years the Hart family seemed happy. Then, in 1898, Fred announced that he was tired of working to support Pearl and their daughter. He said he was joining the army and was going to Cuba to fight the Spanish. Before leaving, he beat Pearl until she was unconscious. Pearl told friends that she hoped Fred Hart would walk into the path of a Spanish bullet.

Pearl either sent or took her little girl to her mother in Lindsay. But if she did go once more to Ontario, she didn't stay long. The West, or at least her romantic idea of it, was in her blood. Early in 1899 Pearl was working as a cook at the Mammoth Mining Camp in Arizona. There she met a miner and would-be desperado who went by the name of Joe Boot. Joe was a handsome, devil-may-care sort of fellow who quickly hit it off with the pretty little camp cook.

Joe said he had a job in the nearby mining town of Globe, and asked Pearl to go there with him. He apparently wanted to marry her, but after her experiences with Fred Hart, Pearl wasn't eager to tie the knot. She did go with Joe to Globe, however, and she got another job as a cook – even though she was getting tired of cooking for "mule-eared miners."

Pearl's family, meanwhile, had moved to Ohio. Her brother sent her a letter saying that their mother was seriously ill. With the high cost of medical care, the family desperately needed money. Pearl became frantic with worry and begged Joe to help. Joe gave Pearl what little money he had. She added her own savings and sent the money to her brother. But it wasn't enough. The family needed more.

Joe tried to make money by setting up a freighting operation, but the business failed. He then tried staking a mining claim, but there was no copper in his stake. Desperate times call for desperate actions. Joe suggested they rob the stagecoach that ran between Globe and the town of Florence.

By that time, stagecoaches were pretty much a thing of the past. Railroads had replaced them almost everywhere. But there still was a stage running between Globe and Florence, 65 miles (100 km) away. Stagecoach passengers were often businessmen who carried traveling money. Moreover, because it had been many years since anyone had robbed a stagecoach, there was nobody riding shotgun. The stickup, Joe said, would be easy.

At first Pearl resisted the idea. Armed robbery seemed to be going a bit too far. Joe insisted that it was the only way to get money for her ailing mother. They could grab hundreds of dollars with a few minutes' work, he said, and make their getaway into New Mexico. Pearl finally turned her back on common sense and agreed to the scheme. She did make Joe promise, though, that nobody would be hurt.

On May 30, 1899, Joe Boot and Pearl Hart waited in ambush at a bend in the dirt track known as the Globe highway. They knew the stage would have to slow down at this spot. Pearl had cut her hair short to make herself look like a boy, and wore a large white sombrero, a man's loose-fitting gray flannel shirt, and a pair of pants. She was armed with a Colt .44 revolver. Joe had a Colt .45. When the stage came rattling around the bend, Joe and Pearl jumped out onto the road. The driver of the two-horse team found himself looking down the barrels of a pair of cocked guns.

"Stop and elevate," Joe commanded.

"Raise 'em," ordered Pearl.

The surprised driver brought the team to such an abrupt halt that the passengers were jolted from their seats and fell to the floor in a heap. The driver could hardly believe what was happening. *Nobody* robbed stage-coaches anymore! While Joe kept the man covered, Pearl took away the man's gun and thrust it into her belt. Then she ordered the startled passengers out of the coach. She held her gun steady as three people, whom she later described as ". . . a short fat man, a dude with his hair parted in the middle, and a pig-tailed Chinaman," climbed out. Pearl held open a sack and said, "Shell out!"

The fat man, who was trembling with fear, dropped in $390. The "dude" contributed $36. The Chinese man had only $5. Pearl took three one-dollar bills from the sack, and gave one to each of the victims "for grub and lodging," she said. Then she told them to get back on board and not look back for 10 minutes. The fat man was so nervous that he tripped and fell on his face as he tried to get back into the coach. The driver cracked his whip, and the coach disappeared down the trail.

Joe and Pearl had the princely sum of $428. What they didn't have was a plan for a getaway. They took to the hills, and soon were completely lost. Joe had read something about outlaws backtracking to confuse anyone chasing them, so he and Pearl backtracked and crisscrossed their own trails, becoming all the more lost.

While Joe and Pearl were stumbling around, the stage arrived in Florence with the incredible news. A stagecoach holdup just like in the bad old days! Sheriff Bill Truman questioned the passengers and driver in his office, and soon knew that the bandits were Joe Boot and Pearl Hart. The driver had recognized Pearl, even in her male getup. Sheriff Truman got a posse together and went after them.

News of the robbery spread across Arizona like wildfire. Not only had there been an old-fashioned stagecoach holdup, but also one of the outlaws was a *woman*! Arizonans were almost proud. Even Texas couldn't boast of a lady road agent.

For three days Joe and Pearl wandered aimlessly, unsure of where to go or what to do. They spent one night in a cave, but first Joe had to shoot the original occupant – a wild pig. Their horses were worn out, so Pearl suggested they steal fresh ones. Joe refused. In the code of the West, a horse thief was considered lower than a snake. The third night they camped out in the open, and were drenched by rain. Someone saw them huddled by their dead fire, and informed the sheriff in Florence.

The next morning the sheriff and his posse surrounded the camp. Joe and Pearl were asleep under a bush. The sheriff crept up and gently slid the outlaws' guns from their holsters. Then he gave Pearl a little poke with the barrel of his rifle and said, "Wake up, Pearl. You're under arrest." Pearl jumped to her feet to find herself disarmed and surrounded by a posse. One of the men awakened Joe with a kick.

"Well," Joe muttered, "we almost made it."

Pearl cursed Joe for being a coward, and scorched the sheriff and his men with some of the roughest language they had ever heard come out of a woman's mouth. "If you hadn't taken my gun," she snarled, "you would never have caught us alive."

Pearl was already playing the role of the Bandit Queen to the hilt, and the sheriff and his men were amused by her performance. But the *Arizona Star* took her seriously. "She is a wildcat of a woman, and had she not been relieved of her guns a bloody foray might have resulted," the paper said.

The prisoners were taken back to Florence, where Pearl found that she was an instant celebrity. Reporters wanted her story, and she told them all about her sick mother and her desperate need for money. "That letter drove me crazy," she told them. "I had no money. I could get no money. From what I now know, I believe I became temporarily insane."

The press and the public ate up Pearl's tale of woe. She said that the robbery had been her idea, not poor sweet Joe's. Like any decent outlaw, she was worried about her horse, and pleaded with her jailers to take good care of it. Newspapers across the country carried her story, quoted her, and sympathized with her. People traveled to the jail to see the real, live, lady outlaw and to get her autograph. Photographers had her pose with pistols and rifles, looking every inch a Bandit Queen.

Then Pearl suddenly took up the cause of women. The women of Arizona did not yet have the right to vote. Pearl told them to fight for their rights. "I shall not consent to be tried under a law which my sex had no voice in making," she declared. The *Arizona Star* newspaper supported her.

Then, Pearl decided to throw a little melodrama into her act. With a deputy looking on, she cried out that life was no longer worth living, tossed some powder into her mouth, and collapsed. She rolled around on the floor, moaning as though in great pain. A doctor examined the apparently dying woman briefly, and then said, "Get up, Pearl, and stop pretending. No one ever killed themselves by swallowing talcum powder."

All the publicity and drama was annoying the sheriff, so he arranged to have Pearl transferred to the jail in Tucson. A reporter for the *Phoenix Republican* wrote, "For this trip, skirts and a hat were provided for Miss Hart. She proved not as good looking a girl as she had been as a boy."

In Tucson Pearl's meals were brought to her by a man named Ed Hogan. He was doing 30 days in jail for being drunk and disorderly. Ed soon fell in love with the lady bandit, and she seemed to return the feeling. Two days before he was due to be released, Hogan told Pearl he was going to escape and wanted her to come with him. Pearl said no, but Hogan persisted. He said they could put together an outlaw gang with her as its queen. Pearl couldn't resist *that*! That night, Hogan used a chisel to cut a hole in the plaster wall so they could escape. They had some trouble getting Pearl's rather ample backside through the hole, but they finally made it to the outside.

The daring escape of the Bandit Queen caused a great sensation. While the sheriff back in Florence assured newspapermen that Pearl would soon be caught, the public admiration for her only increased. Before a month was out, Pearl and Ed were captured in a New Mexico outlaw hangout. Once again, Pearl had disguised herself as a boy. The two had actually been recruiting men for a bandit gang. Now the citizens of New Mexico were thrilled that they had the celebrated lady bandit in their midst.

The next day at the station a crowd of admirers gathered to see Pearl board the train for Tucson. She told them that she and Hogan had been chained together on the floor of a wooden shack when they were captured. "Gawd!" she exclaimed "That's worse than being married."

While most people sympathized with Pearl, there were some who didn't believe her story about robbing the stage to help her sick mother. Then a letter arrived at Sheriff Truman's office from Pearl's brother-in-law. It stated that Mrs. Taylor was indeed suffering from heart disease, and that the family was keeping the news of Pearl's trouble with the law from her. The letter also said that Pearl would be welcomed home if she could be returned to the bosom of her family. Unfortunately for Pearl, there was that little matter of highway robbery.

When Joe Boot and Pearl went on trial, Pearl's lawyer tried to gain sympathy for Pearl by explaining about her sick mother. He also told the jury that this was the young woman's first offence and pleaded with them to acquit her. The all male jury, full of admiration for the Bandit Queen, was reluctant to send a woman to prison. The men took only 10 minutes to find her not guilty. The judge was furious. He blasted the jury, then had them removed and replaced with 12 other men.

Pearl could not be tried again for the stagecoach robbery, so she was tried for stealing the driver's gun. This time the judge warned the jury that they must forget the fact that Pearl was a woman. The jury found Pearl guilty, and the judge sentenced her to five years "to cure her of the habit of robbing stagecoaches." Joe Boot was found guilty of highway robbery and was sentenced to 30 years.

Pearl began serving her sentence, but the prison had no facilities for women. Pearl had to be kept in an area separate from the male inmates. Guards, fascinated by her story, were always finding excuses to visit her. Newspapermen, photographers, and even tourists bombarded the warden with requests to see the lady bandit. Some wanted her to pose in the jail yard dressed in outlaw gear and armed to the teeth.

Meanwhile, Pearl took up religion. She began to lecture her fellow inmates on the evils of crime. She made statements from her jail cell, warning mothers to keep a close eye on their daughters. Everyone seemed to think that Pearl had reformed. The citizens of Arizona began to petition for her release. After serving less than half of her five-year sentence, Pearl Hart was paroled, on the condition that she leave the state. There was gossip that Pearl was let out early because she was pregnant, and the warden and the governor wanted to avoid a scandal.

Pearl showed up next in New Mexico, where her sister, a Mrs. Frizzell, was involved in theatrical productions. Mrs. Frizzell wrote a play, titled

Arizona Bandit, based on Pearl's adventure as an outlaw. Pearl played herself on stage, but was not much of an actress, and the show soon closed.

Pearl next popped up in Kansas City. There she was arrested for being in possession of some stolen canned food. She was using the name Mrs. L.P. Keele, but when the police chief threatened to send her photograph back to the prison in Arizona, Pearl confessed that she was the famous lady bandit. Now the Kansas City reporters swarmed around her, wanting her to tell the tale of her daring robbery all over again. Pearl decided to try writing, and composed a long poem about the event. It went, in part:

> The sun was shining brightly
> On a pleasant afternoon.
> My partner speaking lightly said the stage would be here soon.
> We saw it coming around the bend and called to them to halt.
> Then to their pockets we did attend.
> If they got hurt, twas their own fault.

The Kansas police let Pearl go, and her poem was published in the *Yuma Sun*.

After that, Pearl seems to have vanished. One story says she joined Buffalo Bill Cody's Wild West Show. Another story says Pearl married an Arizona rancher and settled down to an honest life. Still another tale says she ran a cigar store in Kansas City for many years. No one is certain of where the lady bandit went or when she died.

Pearl Hart was the last person to rob a stagecoach, and the only woman ever known to have done so. After that, the girl from small-town Ontario seems to have ridden off into the Wild West sunset of her dreams.

8

Cassie Chadwick

Lady of the Hypnotic Eye

There's an old saying that states, "There's a sucker born every minute." Suckers are considered stupid for being tricked out of money easily by someone more clever. But what if the suckers are successful and respected financial men – bankers, for instance – and the person who swindled them is a woman? A woman who pulled off gigantic swindles in the days when women were only supposed to be concerned with home and family?

Elizabeth (Cassie) Bigley was born in 1856 or '57 and raised on a farm near Eastwood, Ontario, not far from the town of Woodstock. Her father was a former railroad worker. He was not rich, but he provided a comfortable living for his wife and children. Cassie, however, liked money. She liked all the nice things money could buy, like clothing and jewelry. One of her sisters would later say that even as a child, Cassie had a talent for getting other people's money.

One day when she was only 11 or 12, she walked into a barbershop in Brantford, Ontario, and told the barber to cut her long hair short and make her a fake mustache. Then she tried to sell him a gold watch. The suspicious barber sent for the police, who contacted Cassie's father. Her father took her home, but a year later Cassie was arrested for forgery and fraud for trying to pass herself off as heiress to a fortune. The court acquitted her on grounds of insanity. Cassie soon disappeared, and was not seen in Woodstock for another 10 years.

Cassie's exact movements during those 10 years are difficult to trace, but it seems that in 1879 or 1880, she went to Cleveland, Ohio. There, once again posing as a rich woman, she married Dr. Wallace Springsteen. Within days of the wedding, Dr. Springsteen discovered the truth about his new bride and had the marriage dissolved. Cassie then married another Cleveland man and had a son, Emil. Her husband died a few years later, leaving Cassie a respectable estate of $30,000. If she had invested the money wisely, she could have had a decent home for herself and her son. But for Cassie, money was for spending, and she needed more of it.

She soon fell in with a man called Lamb, and for the next few years went under the name of Madam Lydia De Vere. The two traveled around Ohio and sometimes visited New York City, pulling swindle after swindle. Sometimes they got their money through forgery. Sometimes they convinced wealthy men that Cassie was an heiress to whom they could safely lend large sums of cash. Stories also say that Cassie passed herself off as a sort of fortune-teller. People said Cassie was a ladylike person, a very persuasive talker, and that she had "eyes of almost hypnotic brilliancy." In 1889, Cassie visited her family in Woodstock. She seemed to be wealthy, and said she intended to build a little house there and settle down with her son. But within a few months Cassie was in Toledo, Ohio, again tricking people as the mysterious Madam De Vere. But this time she and Lamb were caught.

Lamb was released because it was clear that he was simply Madam De Vere's puppet. He claimed that she had hypnotized him, as she had almost every man from whom she wanted money. Cassie was sentenced to 10 years in the Ohio State Penitentiary, but was pardoned after serving only three-and-a-half years. She was ordered to keep regular appointments with a parole officer in the prison. For a while she did. Then she disappeared again. The state of Ohio was no doubt glad to see the last of Madam Lydia De Vere.

Then in 1897 Dr. Leroy Chadwick of Cleveland, a widower with a daughter, met and married Cassie, the widow with a son. Cassie was good looking, charming, and quite the gracious lady, which the doctor appreciated. Dr. Chadwick had money, which Cassie appreciated even more. But even the high income of the good doctor could not satisfy Cassie's enormous appetite for fine clothes, jewelry, and luxurious living. Before long, Cassie hit on the scheme that would make her one of the most notorious con artists in American and Canadian history.

Not long after her marriage to Chadwick, the story goes, Cassie took a trip to New York City and signed in to the elegant Holland House Hotel. There she managed to "accidentally" bump into an acquaintance of her husband, a lawyer named Dillon. Cassie asked Mr. Dillon if he would be so kind as to escort her to her father's house. Dillon agreed, and hailed an open carriage. Cassie gave the driver an address, and Dillon was astounded when the carriage turned into the gate of the mansion belonging to Andrew Carnegie, one of the richest men in the United States. As Dillon sat dumbfounded, Cassie stepped from the carriage and knocked on the door. When a butler answered, Cassie walked right into the house. Dillon's mind must have been reeling. *Who* could Mrs. Chadwick's father *be?*

Inside the house, Cassie told the startled butler that she wanted to speak to the head housekeeper. When that woman presented herself, Cassie told her that she was thinking of hiring a maid who had supposedly worked in the Carnegie household. Cassie told the woman she was just checking out the girl's references. She gave the housekeeper a name she had made up. Of course, the housekeeper had never heard of the girl in question. Cassie asked more questions, said she must have been misled, apologized for the intrusion, and left. As she went out the door, she turned and waved good-bye. She had managed to stretch her visit in the front hall of the Carnegie house to just under half an hour.

When Cassie climbed back into the waiting carriage, she "accidentally" dropped an unfolded piece of paper. Dillon picked it up for her. He could not help but see that it was a promissory note for two million dollars — signed by Andrew Carnegie himself!

With a great show of false embarrassment, Cassie told the lawyer that she was the illegitimate daughter of the famous Carnegie, and that out of guilt and a sense of fatherly responsibility, "Daddy" gave her lots of money. She said she had other notes just like this one stashed in a dresser drawer at home. She also managed to drop the little bombshell that when "Daddy" passed on, she would inherit 400 million dollars. Cassie told Dillon that he wasn't to tell *anyone* about her big Carnegie secret. Naturally, when he got back to Cleveland, Dillon told everyone he knew in the city's financial circles.

Word was soon being passed among the rich people of Cleveland – and elsewhere – that Mrs. Cassie Chadwick was Carnegie's child and heir. She didn't have to ask bankers for money. They invited her in and opened the vaults for her. They encouraged her to put those valuable promissory notes into safety deposit boxes. Then they happily loaned Cassie huge sums of money – at high rates of interest, of course. But what was their little slice of profit compared to the Carnegie fortune, which was enough to run a whole country?

Meanwhile, Andrew Carnegie had no idea that a woman from small-town Ontario was using his name and forged signature to live an extravagant lifestyle. Nobody wanted to bother the great man over the little matter of a few hundred thousand dollars. They would never think of embarrassing him by checking into his "secret."

Cassie Chadwick rubbed shoulders with the cream of high society. Her home was a mansion in the most fashionable district of Cleveland. She entertained friends with dinners and parties that cost thousands of dollars. She chartered private railway cars for trips to New York City, where she shopped in the best stores and took groups of friends to Broadway shows. It was nothing for her to give gifts of costly jewelry or expensive pianos and organs. Once a year she went to Europe to shop in Paris and Belgium. She almost always paid in cash, but sometimes she asked for credit. Everyone believed that the fine lady who was said to be the daughter of Andrew Carnegie was good for the money. With one exception.

On a 1902 visit to her native Canada, Cassie paid cash for several thousand dollars worth of jewels in an exclusive Toronto shop. Then her eye fell on a gorgeous $10,000 diamond chain. That, she said, she would take on credit. The shop owner politely but firmly said he would have to see madam's money first. Cassie stomped out of the shop without the diamond chain.

Cassie partially repaid loans by borrowing money from other banks, using her "father's" promissory note trick. Investigators later found notes in bank safety deposit boxes in Cleveland and New York City totaling 28 million dollars. Not one of them was worth a penny.

For several years Cassie Chadwick reigned as the queen of Cleveland society. No one, not even her husband, questioned where the money was coming from. Everyone took her word that she was an heiress. All those unpaid portions of loans and bills were mounting up, but Cassie wasn't worried. There was always money available for the daughter of Andrew Carnegie.

In the spring of 1904, Cassie met a Boston banker named Herbert B. Newton, and borrowed $190,000 from him. All was still well with Cassie Chadwick's dream world. That world, however, was about to come crashing down. Cassie was slow in making payments to the Boston bank, and Herbert Newton started an investigation into the financial affairs of Mrs. Cassie Chadwick. Once all the information was in, he was horrified to see the huge amounts of money Cassie had borrowed from banks. When all the arithmetic was done, he could see that Cassie was well over a million dollars in debt. (And a million dollars a century ago would be many times that amount today.) Newton immediately asked to be repaid the loan his bank had made for $190,000. Cassie didn't have it. Newton filed a lawsuit against her. By November 2, 1904, the word was out.

Bank managers in Cleveland and other Ohio cities, as well as in New York City, scrambled to recover their losses. They had to close their doors because so many people wanted to withdraw their own money before the banks collapsed. The Citizens National Bank of Oberlin, Ohio, which had loaned Cassie $800,000, was forced to close for good. Cassie told bank officials, lawyers, and the press that it was all a mistake. She would make good on the loans, she said. She swore she had done nothing wrong. "I would not like to live a minute if I did not think I could pay these poor people back," she said.

The story was carried in newspapers around the world. The Toronto *Globe* called Cassie "The Lady of the Hypnotic Eye." When the bomb exploded, Dr. Chadwick was in Europe with his daughter. He quickly arranged passage to New York. Cassie, meanwhile, fled her Cleveland mansion and checked into a posh New York hotel. It would be her last fling with luxury. She was arrested there on numerous charges of fraud and conspiracy to commit fraud. Jail was her home now. The woman who had spent between 10 and 20 million dollars in a few short years could not raise the $35,000 bail set by the court.

Throughout November and December, the press had a field day with the sensational story. Lists were published of all the banks Cassie had tricked. "I am either an awful dupe or a terrible fool," one bank manager groaned. There were stories that Cassie must have had inside help from tellers or even from men in high positions. Surely, people thought, this colossal fraud could not have been pulled off by one person, and a *woman* at that!

Dr. Chadwick was arrested as his wife's accomplice when his ship docked at New York. The charges were soon dropped for lack of evidence. But people were demanding their money back and poor Dr. Chadwick lost his house and his personal savings – money he had expected to leave to his daughter.

And what about Andrew Carnegie? Was he indeed the father of Cassie Chadwick? The tycoon said, in a simple statement issued by his secretary, that he had never heard of Mrs. Cassie Chadwick, and had not signed a promissory note of any kind in more than 30 years.

Things went from bad to worse for Cassie. She was in debt for tens of thousands of dollars to jewelers and other merchants in New York, Paris, and Belgium. All of them were howling for her blood. (The Toronto jeweler who had refused to extend her credit smugly told the Toronto *Globe* that *he* hadn't fallen under the influence of her hypnotic eye.) Cassie had not declared all of the jewelry she had purchased outside the United States, so she also faced charges of smuggling.

Tales and stories circulated, many of them appearing in the press: Cassie had been seen in the offices of the law firm that handled Andrew Carnegie's affairs; Cassie had more than a million dollars stashed away; Cassie had been planning one more big deal and was preparing to escape to Europe when the law suddenly closed in. In that age, when women always were respectfully called Miss or Mrs., newspaper headlines began to refer to the now infamous adventuress simply as "Cassie."

Cassie Chadwick was taken back to Cleveland to stand trial. Crowds waiting at the train station hooted and jeered her. People in Cleveland were now making connections between Cassie and the mysterious Madam De Vere of more than a decade before. Her fancy mansion and most of what was in it had been seized, but Cassie was escorted there and allowed to select no more than $500 worth of her personal property. She tried to claim nearly $5,000 worth of dresses. Dr. Chadwick was present at the time, and she pleaded her innocence to him. His response was cool. "I hope you will be able to disprove the charges against you," he said.

Cassie Chadwick went on trial in March 1905. She was found guilty on seven charges and sentenced to 10 years in prison. Six other charges were still pending. Her lawyer tried to have her sentences suspended, but failed. When Cassie fully understood that she was going to prison, she became hysterical.

As it turned out, Cassie's prison stay was not a long one. On October 10, 1907, she died in the Ohio State Penitentiary. The headline in the Toronto *Globe* read: "Ontario Girl Who Caused a Sensation in Financial Circles Three Years Ago Dies Far From Any Friend in a Foreign Prison."

It had been a long climb from a small Ontario town to the heights of American society. And in the end, it was a hard fall from a life of luxury, spun around lies, to the hard cold truth of a prison cell.

9

Martha Black

First Lady of the Yukon

artha Purdy was in Seattle, Washington, when she read the letter. She was stunned. Her husband, Will, had changed his mind! There was half a million dollars worth of gold waiting for them in the Yukon Territory. Martha, her brother George, and four other men were just waiting for Will to join them for the long journey north. Martha had already paid for her passage to Skagway, Alaska, on the steamer *Utopia*. Now Will had chickened out! His letter said he had heard terrible things about the Yukon – stories of the cold, hunger, and lawlessness. He didn't want to go there, and he certainly didn't think it was any place for a woman. Wouldn't Martha rather go with him on a voyage to the Sandwich Islands (now Hawaii)?

That summer of 1898, it seemed that the whole world was in the grip of gold fever. Gold had been discovered in the Yukon, a Canadian place most Americans like Martha had never heard of before. There were stories about people picking up fortunes in gold dust and nuggets along streams with exotic names such as the Klondike River and Bonanza Creek. It was a tough place to get to, way up in the frozen Arctic. But if you could make the journey, people said, you'd definitely get rich.

Thousands of would-be prospectors were leaving their homes and jobs to go on an adventure that guaranteed a pot of gold at the end of the rainbow. Not since the California Gold Rush of 1849 had there been such a stampede of treasure seekers. Martha herself had left her two young sons with her parents on a ranch in Kansas. Just a few weeks earlier, Will had been eager go north. Now he was backing out, asking her to go to a tropical island instead. Martha was angry. She wrote back and told him she was going, as planned, to the Yukon! She never saw Will again, and eventually divorced him.

Martha had always been a determined person and she wasn't afraid of hardship once she made her mind up to do something. But on that June day, she could hardly have guessed that she was setting out on an adventure that would last almost 60 years.

She was born Martha Louise Munger in 1866, in Chicago. Her father was a successful businessman, and Martha and her younger brother George had a privileged upbringing. When she was five, her parents were almost ruined by the Great Chicago Fire, and the family was forced to live for a time in the refugee camp known as Poverty Flats. But with hard work and their shrewd business sense, the Mungers were able to regain their fortune and their place in society. For the remainder of her childhood, Martha enjoyed the best of everything.

Since she was so lively and a bit of a prankster, her parents sent her to a Roman Catholic convent school, where they hoped the nuns would teach her some self-discipline. Martha was happy at school and learned all the things considered essential for a proper young lady of her time – needlework, elocution, music, deportment, riding, tennis, and botany, a subject that would become a lifelong passion.

After her graduation, Martha fell in love with handsome, young Will Purdy, son of the president of the Chicago Rock Island and Pacific Railway. They soon married and had two sons. Their house was a wedding gift from Martha's father, and the families of both newlyweds furnished it for them. Will's father gave him an easy, well-paid job.

For 10 years Martha lived the life of a socialite. She gave and attended dinner parties, shopped for fine clothes, and devoted some of her time to public charities. She loved her children, and for a time she thought she loved Will. But Martha was growing bored. For someone who craved adventure and new experiences, life was becoming downright dull. Money just wasn't buying her happiness.

Then came the news of gold in the Klondike. Everyone was abuzz. Will wanted to go. So did Martha's brother George. And this was just the sort of thing Martha had been waiting for. She announced that she was going, too. The idea of a trip to the wild Canadian North became all the more exciting when a friend of Will's father, Mr. Lambert, told them about a million dollars' worth of gold dust sitting in Dawson City, the booming new capital of the Yukon. He said that his uncle had struck it rich up there, but then died, leaving the money to him. Lambert said he was willing to split the gold fifty-fifty with anyone who would go and get it. Half a million! And they wouldn't even have to dig it out of the ground or pan it out of a river! Martha and George and some friends headed west, making a stop in Denver, where Martha bought the clothes she thought she would need for the expedition. Then, as they waited for Will to join them in Seattle, the letter came. The Yukon was a scary place, Will said. He would rather go on a pleasure cruise to the Sandwich Islands.

When George Munger learned that his sister was determined to go to the Yukon without her husband, he tried to persuade her to go back home. But Martha was pretty persuasive herself, and when the *Utopia* sailed, Martha was aboard. The ship was crowded with men who spent most of their time gambling and drinking. Martha had to share her cabin with a gambler and his mistress, and a strange character known only as "Birdie." Surprisingly, Martha liked these unusual people. And though the sea voyage was rough, she fell in love with the rugged beauty of the British Columbia and Alaska coastlines as the ship pushed northward toward the Land of the Midnight Sun.

After seven days at sea, the *Utopia* docked at Skagway, Alaska. It was a ramshackle, bustling port run entirely by criminals. Killers and swindlers preyed on travelers heading for the Yukon. Murder and robbery were everyday events. Martha and the men didn't waste much time in Skagway.

Their route to Dawson took them to the town of Dyea, where they stayed two weeks, making arrangements for the transportation of their supplies. Martha collected wildflowers and wrote to her parents, expressing her loneliness for them and her children. She was the cook for the little group, and quickly learned how to make sourdough – bread or pancakes made without yeast. It was such a big part of the diet that people who had spent a winter in the North became known as "sourdoughs." Martha also learned to improvise. The pan in which she mixed her dough also was used as a dishpan and as a bathtub. Once they left Dyea, they faced the hardest leg of the journey – the hike through the steep, dangerous Chilkoot Pass, which linked Alaska to the Yukon.

The Chilkoot Pass was a narrow trail going almost straight up to a summit, and then almost straight down the other side. Its base on the American side was littered with dead horses and rubbish. Just looking up the 3,500-foot (1,067-meter) trail to the top was enough to make many turn back. Every bit of food and every piece of equipment had to be carried in backpacks. Martha's party hired Native packers for the job, but even so, the climb was an ordeal she would never forget. Years later she wrote in her autobiography, "In my memory it will ever remain a hideous nightmare. The trail led through a scrub pine forest where we tripped over bare roots of trees that curled over and around rocks and boulders like great devilfishes. Rocks! Rocks! Rocks! Tearing boots to pieces. Hands bleeding with scratches. I can bear it no longer. In my agony, I beg the men to leave me – to let me lie in my tracks and stay for the night."

Like most of the gold rushers, Martha had no idea how bad it would be on the trail. The stylish clothing she had bought in Denver was almost useless. Her tight corset, bulky bloomers, and long skirt might have been fine for a walk in a city park, but they were no good on the steep climb.

At last they reached top, which was the international border. There they had to report to the North West Mounted Police. The Mounties were there to collect duties and prevent known criminals from entering the Yukon. They also turned back any who did not have enough provisions to last through the winter. The trip down was just as difficult as the climb up, and Martha's brother had to help her walk the last mile. But when she had completed the 42-mile (68-km) marathon, Martha felt a sense of triumph. "I had actually walked over the Chilkoot Pass! . . . I would never do it again, knowing now what it meant . . . not for all the gold in the Klondyke (sic) . . . And yet, knowing now what it meant, would I miss it? . . . No, never! . . . Not even for all the gold in the world!"

The group rested for two weeks while their baggage and supplies caught up with them. Most of the rest of the trip would be by water, and Martha's party would have to make arrangements for their own boat. They had a dory constructed, and hired a navigator. When the boat was loaded with supplies and passengers, it could barely float. When the group reported to the Mounted Police post at Lake Taglish, they were the 14,405th boat to pass through that summer. Martha was the 631st woman. She was also one of the few women to brave the whitewater ride through Miles Canyon and the treacherous White Horse Rapids. The Mounties always ordered women and children to walk along the bank while the men navigated the foaming waters. But after the Chilkoot Pass, Martha proba-bly figured she had walked enough.

Martha was fascinated by the animals, wildflowers, and Natives she saw. At night her group camped ashore, fished, hunted squirrels, and met fellow travelers from all over the world. The glorious adventure was spoiled only by the mosquitoes. "Bloodthirsty brutes," Martha called them. On August 5, 1898, they rounded a bend in the river and there was the rather rough-looking Dawson City.

The town of wooden buildings and canvas tents sprawled across the flats where the Klondike and Yukon Rivers met. It was a rough frontier town, full of gold rushers, but not as dangerous as Skagway. The Mounties kept bad characters out, and upheld the law. They looked the other way when it came to drinking and gambling, but they acted quickly if anyone committed a violent crime or disturbed the peace. Wrongdoers were escorted to the border and sent packing. This was called being given "a blue ticket to the outside."

Everything in Dawson was expensive. Supplies had to come up the Yukon River from the sea in paddle wheelers, which could only operate during the short summer months. Milk was $4 a quart (equal to $20 or more in today's money). Flour was $1 a pound, apples $1.50 each, and eggs almost worth their weight in gold. Gold dust was used to buy goods. Martha and her companions couldn't afford to buy or build a house in Dawson itself, so they erected a log cabin on the other side of the river. It was on a hillside overlooking a poor collection of shacks and tents known as Lousetown. It was a far cry from the kind of upscale neighborhoods Martha was used to, but she made the little home as comfortable and attractive as she could. She had to learn to do without electricity and indoor plumbing.

Now Martha went into Dawson to find Lambert's million dollars. She was in for a huge disappointment. Everyone she spoke to had to be bribed with money first, which she politely called "tipping." They all said they knew nothing about the gold or Lambert. She finally had to accept the fact that the million dollars' worth of gold dust was gone. What's more, she and her companions were almost broke.

Then Martha dropped another bombshell on the men in her group. She was pregnant! Her brother was furious with her for not telling them before. Their plan had been for Martha to leave Dawson before the freeze-up, but there was no way she could travel back through the Chilkoot Pass in her condition. Martha had to stay on with George and the others. They all staked claims in the gold diggings and prepared to face the long dark Arctic winter.

For Martha the first months were marked by loneliness and depression. She missed her children, and very little mail got in or out of Dawson. In the depth of winter the world was as dark and cold at high noon as it was at midnight. Martha asked about having her baby in the little Dawson hospital, and was told it would cost $1,000 – money she didn't have. On

January 31, 1899, Martha, alone in the cabin, gave birth to a baby boy she named Lyman.

Overnight, Martha and her baby became the most popular people in town. The miners took Lyman to heart and called him "The Little *Cheechako*," a nickname given to newcomers in the Yukon. They came around with gifts of food, clothing, candy, and even gold dust. The little cabin on the wrong side of the river was a happier place. Martha's depression lifted, and her old energy returned.

Then a series of disasters hit Dawson. First, a deadly typhoid epidemic ran through the community. Then Dawson was struck by the worst enemy of wooden towns – fire. The blaze gutted the downtown business section, destroying more than a hundred buildings And just a month later, while the burned-out part of Dawson was being rebuilt, the Little *Cheechako* and his mother were very nearly victims of another disaster. On a warm spring day, Martha was sitting in front of the cabin listening to the crackling and groaning of the ice breakup. The baby was sleeping nearby. Martha was suddenly startled by a rumbling sound coming from above and behind the cabin. She looked up the slope. ". . . to my horror I saw the whole hillside slowly moving toward the cabin. . . ." A landslide! The quick thaw had loosened the earth and made it into a river of mud that was sweeping everything away with it.

"I dashed into the cabin again," she later said. "I seized the baby, wrapped him in a shawl, put on my own coat, and paralyzed with fright, stood at the corner of the cabin, wondering desperately what move to make . . . I knew I was in terrible danger. God answered my prayer. The onrushing avalanche was halted by a small clump of trees, 70 feet above the cabin . . ."

The mud and debris slid down on either side of the cabin, and Martha and the baby were not even touched. A little later in the day, the ice in the river broke up with a great roar. Martha had survived a winter in the Yukon. Now she was a sourdough.

In midsummer Martha was surprised to see her father arrive at the cabin. He had come to take her and the baby home. She didn't want to leave, but George said he would stay and look after their claims. Martha said she would go and stay at home, but if George found gold, she was coming back.

The following year Martha was heading north. George had reported that their claims were producing gold. This time Martha took her oldest son, Warren, with her. Martha had plans – and financial support from her father – to build a sawmill and a quartz mill. She was smart enough to know that the gold bonanza wouldn't last forever. Yukoners would need other businesses in order to survive. While she waited for the equipment to arrive, she worked as a camp cook. Once the mills were operating, Martha hired men to work for her

Dawson City was changing. The Gold Rush was over and the stampeders packed up and headed for a new gold strike at Nome, Alaska. Those who stayed in Dawson were settling into a more normal life. One of them was George Black, a lawyer from New Brunswick who had come to Dawson looking for gold. When he didn't strike it rich, he opened a law office in town. He and Martha married in 1904. The couple shared a love of the Yukon and cared about its future. Martha became a Canadian.

Martha Black was one of Dawson's most prominent citizens. She was a successful businesswoman and had a fine house. She was comfortable with everyone, rich or poor. Indeed, the town's upper class was sometimes shocked that Martha would spend time with dance hall girls and rough miners. She never closed her door to anyone who was cold and hungry – that was the code of the Yukon. But there were some people who did not like her sharp tongue and her proud manner.

In 1911, George was appointed Commissioner for the Yukon Territory, a position similar to that of governor. Martha was now the First Lady of the Yukon. She was the hostess of Government House, though she said that she had been just as comfortable in her log cabin. Her wildflower exhibits were the pride of the North, and she was made an honorary member of the Imperial Order of the Daughters of the Empire.

After the outbreak of World War I, George resigned as Commissioner to establish the Yukon Infantry Company. One of its members was Martha's 17-year-old son, Lyman. When the soldiers traveled to Halifax in 1917 to board a ship for England, Martha went with them. Women were not supposed to travel on troop ships, but Martha pestered and bullied officials until she got permission.

While her husband and all three of her sons were fighting in the trenches in France, Martha did her part for the war effort in England. She worked with the Red Cross, gave lectures to raise funds for the war, and made her London apartment a home-away-from-home for Yukon soldiers on leave. At the war's end in 1918, all three boys and George had survived, though George had been wounded. Lyman was decorated with the Military Cross. All of them were glad to return to Canada.

In the federal election of 1921, George won a seat in Parliament as the Conservative member from the Yukon. He was re-elected three times and then was appointed Speaker of the House. In 1935 illness forced George to give up politics. The Yukon Conservative Party asked Martha, who was then almost 70 years old, to run for election in his place. It was a difficult campaign, but the woman who had trekked through the Chilkoot Pass and given birth alone in the howling wilderness was up to it. Though the Federal Conservative Party lost the election, Martha won her seat for the Yukon. She was only the second woman to be elected to Canada's House of Commons.

Martha carried out her duties faithfully, speaking strongly on issues such as public health and conservation. She even insisted that her old homeland, the United States, foot the whole bill for the construction of the Alaska Highway. All the while she said that she was just "keeping the seat warm for George."

Sadly, within a six-month period in 1937, her brother George and her son Warren died, and Lyman was killed in a car accident. She served out her term in spite of her grief, but the losses weighed heavily upon her. By the time of the next election, her husband was able to campaign again. He won, and held his seat until his retirement from politics in 1949.

In that year Martha was presented with The Order of the British Empire. Her writings on botany had already earned her a Fellowship in the Royal Geographic Society. Since Dawson City was going downhill, she and George moved to the new Territorial Capital at Whitehorse. Martha was confined to a wheelchair because of arthritis, but she continued to receive visitors – even Prince Philip came to call. Martha Black died suddenly on October 31, 1957, at the age of 91. Born American, she had become a Canadian legend in her beloved Yukon.

10

Mina Hubbard

Explorer of Uncharted Labrador

Mina Hubbard was devastated by the news. Her husband, American journalist Leonidas Hubbard, was dead! He and his party had become lost while exploring unmapped areas of Labrador in 1903. Leonidas had starved to death. His two companions – a 'Scotch Indian' named George Elson, from Northern Ontario, and fellow American Dillon Wallace – barely made it back alive. Wallace had been Leonidas Hubbard's close friend. He told the grief-stricken Mrs. Hubbard that he wanted to write a book about the expedition. Mina agreed and Wallace's book, *The Lure of the Labrador Wild*, was based largely on the dead man's journal.

When the book was published, however, Mina Hubbard was very upset. She felt that Wallace had made her husband look like a weak person who was largely responsible for the failure of the expedition. She even decided that Wallace had been responsible for her husband's death. When she learned, in 1905, that Wallace intended to make another attempt at the journey, she decided to restore her husband's good name by making the trip herself.

She said she would travel from the Hudson's Bay Company post at Northwest River, through the Labrador interior, to Ungava Bay. In the early 1900s the press feasted on tales of adventure in the last unexplored corners of the world. Newspaper readers were amazed that a well-to-do white woman would dare to travel in the frigid wilderness. Only Natives had the skills for survival there. Not only that, Mina said that she would reach Ungava Bay ahead of Wallace. She was going to compete with a *man*!

Mina Benson had been born in 1870 in Bewdley, near Hamilton, Ontario. She had a good education, and was trained as a nurse. Mina went to New York City and was working at Staten Island Hospital in 1900 when she met Leonidas Hubbard. He was in the hospital recovering from typhoid fever. They were married early the next year.

Leonidas was very interested in outdoor adventure, but he didn't have much experience. Just two years into their marriage, he decided to go off to explore wild Labrador and make a name for himself. Mina had no objections. But when he was brought back to New York in a coffin, Mina ran away with the idea that Dillon Wallace was responsible for his death, not poor planning and lack of preparation.

Nevertheless, Mina was very careful with her own preparations. She began by hiring four very capable men, though there was no doubt that she was in charge of the expedition. The crew boss was George Elson, who had accompanied her husband and Wallace. Then there were Joe Iserhoff, who was half-Russian and half-Native, and Job Chapries, a Cree. Both men were from the James Bay region. The youngest member of the party was a half-Inuit trapper named Gilbert Blake. He was familiar with some of the country they would travel through. All the men were good strong paddlers who knew how to handle canoes in all kinds of water.

The explorers would have to hunt and fish for most of their food, but they also packed 750 pounds (340 kilograms) of provisions – more than half of it was flour. Their equipment included guns (Mina herself strapped on a revolver), two tents, cooking gear, knives, axes, nets, sleeping bags, two cameras, and a hot water bottle for Mina on cold nights. One of the most important pieces of equipment was a sextant, with which Mina could take daily readings to establish their location.

On June 27, 1905, the party set off in two canoes. Their goal was the Hudson's Bay Company Post on Ungava Bay, more than 500 rugged miles (800 km) away. They had to arrive there by the last week of August to meet up with the Company supply ship *Pelican*. If they missed the ship, they would be stranded there for the long Labrador winter. At about the same time that Mina's expedition got under way, Dillon Wallace began his journey. He had decided to take a more overland route.

The idea of a lone woman traveling through remote country with four men must certainly have raised eyebrows. Mina's companions, however, were always gentlemen. It does seem from Mina's journal that George Elson was falling in love with her, but if that was so, he kept his feelings to himself.

Mina's companions tried their best to keep her out of danger, since she was a woman – the 'weaker sex.' There were times when she found this annoying. "It began to be somewhat irksome to be so well taken care of," she wrote. There were even times, she said, when she wished she were a man, so she could do things women weren't supposed to do, like climb up rocks and trees to look into eagles' nests.

Though she was well prepared and brimming with self-confidence, Mina did not underestimate the raw power of Labrador, as her husband had done. In the remote wilderness the smallest accident or injury can lead to disaster – a fall, an overturned canoe, an encounter with a wild animal. She knew the journey would be a tough one.

The route took them through rivers and lakes, deep into Labrador. Sometimes they paddled. Sometimes Mina walked while the men poled the canoes up stretches of shallow water. Many times they had to portage, carrying canoes and supplies overland to the next body of water. Just a few days into the journey, they had a close brush with disaster. Mina, George, and Gilbert were on shore while Joe and Job were poling a canoe up a wicked rapid. Mina wrote in her journal:

". . . I saw the canoe turn bottom up like a flash, and both men disappeared. I stood unable to move. Almost immediately Joe came up. Then I saw Job appear. He had not been able to hold to the canoe. The current had swept him off, and was now carrying him downriver. My heart sickened at the sight, and still I could not move."

Mina shouted to Joe, who was able to rescue Job from the fast water. George pulled the overturned canoe ashore. They had lost their three axes, necessary tools in the bush. Fortunately, several days later they found an old axe at an abandoned Native camp.

"Starvation broods over Labrador," Mina wrote in her journal. But that slow death was not for her group. Day after day they ate bannock, a type of bread made with flour, water, salt and baking powder. They cooked it over an open fire, so the bannock was often covered with ash. Mina found it to be tough. George joked, "You can throw them around, or sit on them, or jump on them, and they are just as good after you have done it as before."

Mina and the men fished, gathered berries, and hunted. They brought in geese, ptarmigan, partridges, and ducks. Sometimes they had to settle for porcupine, which Mina didn't like at all. When they came upon migrating caribou the men would shoot one, butcher it, and dry the meat to preserve it. Caribou meat helped them survive, but it bothered Mina to see the beautiful animals killed. Once, on Indian House Lake, George caught a swimming caribou by the tail and allowed it to tow the canoe through the water, then let it go unharmed.

The only 'wild' animals to give them trouble were mice, which came in the night to eat holes in things like hats and waterproof bags. Worse than the mice were the flies and mosquitoes. Mina wrote frequently about the biting, stinging hordes:

"My hands and face, too, were swollen and sore from the bites of the flies and mosquitoes . . . I could feel my ears and neck wet and sticky with blood, for some of the bites bled a good deal . . . Their bite was like the touch of a live coal."

The net veil Mina wore to protect her face and the smudge fires the men lit at night were little help against the maddening insects. Sometimes Mina prayed for rain or a sharp cold night to keep the pests away. But the rain brought its own problems. It soaked clothing and made campfires impossible, leaving them cold, wet, and shivering in their tents. Worst of all, a long storm could confine them to camp for days, wasting precious time. They needed to reach Ungava Bay on schedule.

In spite of all the bad weather, hard work, and insects, Mina was absolutely in love with the wild country. She drew maps, made notes, took photographs, and collected specimens of the plants. She filled her journal with descriptions of the rivers, lakes, and mountains. She loved the freedom of the great land so much that she put her foot down and said the men were being too protective of her. She left camp alone to do a little exploring, which probably wasn't a wise thing for *anyone* to do. The four men almost panicked when they realized she was missing, and went searching for her. When they found her, George said that they had never been on a trip before "where the women didn't do what they were told."

By August 11 the expedition had covered 300 miles (480 km) and had reached the source of the river that flows north to Ungava Bay. But many portages around boiling rapids made progress very slow. Time was running out, and they had to reach Ungava Bay before the *Pelican* departed at the end of the month. Now, every hour counted.

They began to come across old camps and Native burial grounds. They were in the country of the Montagnais tribe, and Mina's guides were worried that if they came upon a Native camp, the welcome might not be friendly. A few days later they sighted a Montagnais camp, and the men paddled very slowly as they approached it. They heard rifle shots, and Mina responded by firing her revolver in the air. As they drew nearer they heard children screaming and women shouting. George understood their language and realized they were shouting, "Go away! Go away! We are afraid of you. Our husbands are away."

George answered them in Montagnais. "We are strangers and are passing through your country," he yelled. Suddenly they were welcomed with greetings and laughter. The Montagnais men were away on a trading excursion, so only the women and children were in the camp. Mina took some pictures and made notes on the Native dress and lodgings. The visit had to be short, even though the people tried to persuade the strangers to stay. The Montagnais told Mina and the men that they were two days' travel from the country of the Nascaupee, the "Barren Grounds" tribe. Then, to Mina's distress, the Natives said it would take two more months to reach Ungava Bay. Mina's heart sank. That would mean they had no hope of catching the *Pelican*. She wondered if they should turn around and go back the way they had come, but then they might end up traveling through Labrador in winter. Perhaps the Montagnais were exaggerating. She decided to push on. But what if the Natives were correct?

They reached the country of the Nascaupee tribe in three days. Again they were welcomed. The Nascaupee were very excited at seeing an "English" woman in their country. Mina took more pictures and made more notes. When the Natives heard that the strangers were going to the post on Ungava Bay, they said, "Oh! You are near now. You will sleep only five times if you travel fast."

Only five days to the post! Mina was thrilled. In fact, she was so sure of reaching her goal that she shared some of her provisions with the Nascaupee. Mina gave away some tea, rice, flour, and salt. George, however, thought that the Nascaupee might just be telling them that Ungava was close, so that they would give away more of their provisions. He was also worried about the water ahead. The Natives had told him there were rapids almost all the way to the coast.

They did, in fact, have to travel down over 130 miles (210 km) of almost continuous rapids, at what Mina called "toboggan pace." There was always the danger of a canoe overturning, and the powerful current made it difficult for them to go ashore. While shooting one rapid, George and Job had a narrow escape, almost wrecking their canoe on some rocks.

Finally, on August 26, they reached quiet water. They had to camp when darkness fell, though they were certain they were only a few miles from the Hudson's Bay Company post. The next morning all that was on Mina's mind was the *Pelican*. Had they missed the ship? The men were paddling at a leisurely pace, allowing the river to carry them. Mina wanted them to paddle like demons. She wrote. ". . . my strong desire was to take them by their collars and knock their heads together *hard*. This was not practical in the canoe, however. . . ."

Suddenly George exclaimed, "There it is!" Minutes later they beached the canoes in a cove in front of a little group of tiny buildings. Mina joined the men in their shouts of joy, but she was still a bundle of nerves. She could not see the *Pelican*. When the agent at the post came down to greet them, Mina asked, "Has the ship been here?"

She must have felt the sharp stab of disappointment when he told her it had. "And gone again?" she asked.

The man replied, "Yes. She was here last September. I expect her in September again, about the middle of the month, or later."

The *Pelican*, it turned out, had been unexpectedly delayed. Mina and the four men had made it!

Mina Hubbard was the first non-Native woman to travel through the wilds of Labrador, a remarkable accomplishment at that time. Thanks to her careful planning and her wise choice of guides, she had done it without any major problems. Her expedition gained valuable information on the geography, flora, wildlife, and people of the region. She was the first person to photograph the Natives of the interior. And to top it all off, she won her race with Dillon Wallace. She arrived at the post six weeks ahead of him. Yet the most important thing to her, she wrote, was that she had in a small way fulfilled her late husband's dream.

A few years after her great adventure, Mina traveled to England to promote her book, *A Woman's Way Through Unknown Labrador*. There she married again, and apparently lived a quiet life. In 1956, at the age of 86 and suffering from dementia, Mina Hubbard wandered into the path of a train and was killed. Her book remains a Canadian classic.

11

Florence Lassandro

The Mobster Princess

She liked fast cars, guns, and bootleggers. Florence Lassandro was a real Roaring Twenties mobster princess. If Florence had lived her short life in the United States, there probably would be a Hollywood film about her, complete with car chases and gunfire.

She was born Filumena Costanzo in Calabria, a dry, poor part of Italy, about 1901. When she was 9 years old, Filumena's family joined the thousands of other Italians who were migrating to North America. Her family eventually settled in Fernie, British Columbia. Many Italians went to that area because there were jobs in the Crowsnest Pass, the mountain crossing that links British Columbia to Alberta. There is a story that one of Filumena's teachers had difficulty pronouncing her name, and so called her Florence. The teacher told the young girl that the name meant "Flowers," and since Filumena loved flowers she happily accepted her new name.

School days were soon finished for Florence; her parents had arranged a marriage for her. She did not want to marry Carlo Sanfidele, the man they had chosen. She was 14, he was 23. She was attractive, he was not. But Florence had to follow her parents' wishes. So in 1915 she went to the altar with a man she would never learn to love. He was a dull, perhaps even abusive, husband. The teenaged Florence was sure she could have done better for herself. Ironically, it was through Carlo that Florence met Emilio Picariello, the man who would share her sad appointment with destiny.

Emilio Picariello had arrived in Toronto from Sicily at the turn of the century. Sometime before World War I, he took his wife and their children west and settled in Fernie, where he got a job in a macaroni factory. Picariello was an ambitious man, with a sharp nose for business. Soon he was selling ice cream, peanuts, and cigars. He also made money by collecting discarded bottles. In 1918 he bought the Alberta Hotel in Blairmore, Alberta, and became the agent for a Lethbridge brewery. In 1915 Albertans voted in favor of prohibition, banning the manufacture, transportation, and sale of alcohol. The Alberta Hotel soon became a front for one of the biggest bootlegging operations in the West. Picariello was bringing alcohol illegally into Alberta through the Crowsnest Pass. Eventually he controlled a whiskey empire that included much of southern Alberta and British Columbia, as well as parts of Montana and Idaho.

Emperor Pic, as he came to be known, became a godfather figure to the Italian people of the region. He gave food and other gifts to the needy and put on movie shows for children. He was the man to go to if you had a problem. He was a jolly character who kept a bear cub and a wolf cub as pets. He had himself elected to the Blairmore town council. At the height of his power, Emperor Pic was said to be worth more than $200,000 — several millions in today's currency.

Because Florence's husband, Carlo, worked for Picariello, she got to know Carlo's boss, as well as the boss's family. Florence quickly took a liking to them. Shortly after Carlo and Florence were married, they moved to Pennsylvania. There Carlo went to work for Italian gangsters associated with Picariello. Within a year Carlo and Florence were back in Canada, but because of an immigration problem they had changed their name. They were now Charles and Florence Lassandro.

Emperor Pic kept a fleet of six big McLaughlin Buicks for running alcohol from place to place. The cars were fast, had reinforced front bumpers for crashing police roadblocks, and had room for dozens of cases of liquor. He called his cars the Whiskey Six. When the Lassandros returned from Pennsylvania, the Emperor gave Carlo the job of keeping his fleet in good working order. Soon Florence was working for Picariello, too, transporting illegal alcohol.

Sometimes Florence went on these rum-running trips as a passenger, with Emperor Picariello or his teenaged son, Steve, driving. It looked innocent, like a man and his daughter or two young lovers out for a ride. The bootleggers believed that the police would not shoot at a car with a woman in it.

Florence, however, was not content to be just a passenger. By 1919 she was driving the big Whiskey Six cars herself. Very few women drove at all in those days. Driving an automobile was considered "man's work." But Florence, still in her teens, was roaring down the highways and along mountain back roads, playing cat and mouse with the police. And those who saw her at the wheel said that Florence could *really* drive – better than the men, some said.

Bootlegging was a dangerous business. There was the constant threat of being caught by the police or hijacked by other criminals. Florence always carried a .38 caliber revolver in her purse. Maybe it was for safety, or maybe she toted a gun just because she found it thrilling to be an outlaw. For Florence it was literally life in the fast lane, with plenty of high-speed excitement and lots of money.

Eventually Florence left Carlo and went to live with the Picariello family. If anyone asked, she said she was their housekeeper. She and Pic's wife, Maria, were apparently the best of friends. But gossips whispered that she was Emperor Pic's mistress. Others believed she was romantically involved with Steve Picariello, who was only a little younger than she was.

Emperor Pic's main problem was the Alberta Provincial Police (APP), a force that had been created especially to deal with bootleggers. The officers would set up checkpoints on highways near the Montana border and the British Columbia provincial line to catch cars taking liquor into

Alberta. To fool the police, Emilio Picariello would send a scout car ahead of the cars carrying booze. If the scout driver spotted a police check, he would turn around and go back to warn the others. Then they could dash back to safety. Or Picariello would send a decoy car ahead. While the police were searching the decoy, the cars carrying the alcohol would slip past. Young Steve and Florence often rode decoy.

Like other bootleggers, Emperor Pic used bribes and payoffs to get policemen to look the other way. It was no secret that when certain officers wanted liquor for parties of their own, Picariello supplied it. There was an unwritten agreement, or so Emperor Pic thought, that neither side would use violence. He seemed to believe that the business could be carried on without a lot of unnecessary shooting. But all across the continent the bootleg trade was drawing violence like a magnet.

One police officer who did not believe in going easy on the bootleggers was Constable Stephen Lawson. Originally from England, he was a well respected and experienced cop. Just six months after joining the APP, Lawson received a tip that Emilio and Steve Picariello, and a man named McAlpine, were heading for Coleman, Alberta, in three cars loaded with alcohol from British Columbia. Emperor Pic was actually in an empty decoy car, while McAlpine and 18-year-old Steve drove the rumrunners. Lawson saw the cars roll through Coleman, but did not try to stop them. He telephoned ahead to the town of Frank, and passed the word to the APP station there. Two officers were sent to the Alberta Hotel in Blairmore, hoping to catch Emperor Pic when he unloaded his cargo.

The Whiskey Sixes were indeed there when the officers roared up to the hotel, but when Picariello saw the police, he acted swiftly. He leaned on his horn, warning Steve. The youngster sped away in the car still loaded with cases of whiskey. He was heading through the Pass for the safety of British Columbia. When the police began to give chase, Emperor Pic blocked the road with his own car. The officers managed to get around it, but by then they had little chance of overtaking Steve's powerful car. They phoned ahead to Constable Lawson to tell him Steve Picariello was trying to escape to B.C. with a carload of whiskey.

As Steve came thundering down the highway, Constable Lawson stood out on the road with his hand raised in a clear signal for the young bootlegger to stop. Steve kept the pedal to the floor and at the last moment swerved around the policeman. Lawson fired a couple of warning shots, but the car kept going. Lawson and another officer jumped in a car and screeched off in pursuit. Lawson leaned out the window and fired several shots at the fleeing rumrunners, trying to blow out a tire. He did not know that one of his bullets had struck Steve in the hand. It was only a slight injury, but one that was to become important.

Steve drove on in spite of his bloodied hand, but the constables blew a tire and had to stop. While they were changing the tire at the side of the road, Picariello pulled up in his car. Lawson and Emperor Pic exchanged words, with the constable allegedly telling Emilio, "You had better bring your son back, because if you don't get him, I'll go and get him." Picariello shrugged and drove off.

Sometime later a sergeant named Scott encountered Picariello near Coleman. There were no witnesses, but according to Scott, Emperor Pic said, "If Lawson shot Steve, I would kill him." Months later, in court, a witness would testify that Picariello repeated that threat to others that very day, and then kissed the gun he always carried.

What followed was a confusion of misinformation, mixed signals, and bad judgment. Steve Picariello arrived safely in Fernie, but his father didn't know that and wasn't sure what had happened to him. He wanted to get his son, and the carload of whiskey, back into Alberta with no further trouble from the police. He sent someone to Fernie to look for the boy. Then he received an anonymous phone call telling him that Steve had been shot. No one knows just what the Emperor was told. He may have thought that Steve was dead or seriously wounded, or perhaps he knew that Steve was only slightly hurt but was enraged that a cop had taken some potshots at his boy. After all, the bootlegging game was supposed to be bloodless on Emperor Pic's turf. He allegedly said, "I don't like this shooting business, but if they are going to shoot, I can shoot, too." And, "If he has shot my boy, I'll kill every policeman in the Pass, by God!"

Emilio Picariello decided to confront Constable Lawson, perhaps even make the officer accompany him to Fernie to find out just what kind of shape Steve was in. Florence Lassandro volunteered to go with him because, as she said later, she was "fond of Steve." Each was armed with a .38 caliber pistol.

The Whiskey Six McLaughlin, with Picariello driving, pulled up in front of the APP station in Blairmore, which was also where Constable Lawson lived with his wife and children. Lawson came out of the house, unarmed, to see what the bootleggers wanted. He stood with one foot resting on the running board, talking with Emperor Pic through the open driver's window. Picariello was furious with him for shooting at young Steve. Lawson said that he had shot at the tires. Picariello demanded that Lawson go to Fernie with him. Lawson refused.

Then for some reason – maybe Picariello had drawn his gun – Lawson leaned in the window and started wrestling with Picariello. Three or four shots rang out. Two of them damaged the interior of the car without hurting anyone. But one hit Constable Lawson in the back as he tried to get away from the car. He fell to the ground and died within minutes. Among the several witnesses was his 9-year-old daughter, Pearl. She would testify later, ". . . the lady shot and then the man shot and then they shot again . . . and Daddy fell down." But there would also be testimony that the shot that killed Lawson did not come from the car at all, but from an alley by the house.

Florence and Picariello fled the scene. Witnesses had recognized him, but not Florence. Several of them, including Pearl Lawson, told police that Picariello's female accomplice was wearing a red tam.

The next day the police caught Emperor Pic as he tried to run for the hills on foot. He told them that Florence Lassandro had been in the car with him when Lawson was shot. Sergeant Scott arrested Florence at the home of a friend, without any trouble. She had a red tam, and a button found in Picariello's car matched the ones on her coat. There were .38 caliber cartridges in her coat pocket. This was only circumstantial evidence, but in the Blairmore police station Florence "confessed" – or so Sergeant Scott would testify.

As Scott listened to her *without writing anything down*, Florence said that she had panicked and shot Constable Lawson in self-defense. But how could it have been self-defense when Lawson was unarmed?

Florence and Emperor Pic went on trial on November 22, 1922, in Calgary. One of Alberta's best criminal lawyers fought hard for Picariello and Florence, trying to convince the jury that a shot from the alley had killed Lawson. Sergeant Scott's testimony, he said, was hearsay. He tried to portray Florence as a "poor little girl" who had fallen in with bad company. But there were many outside factors at work during that sensational trial.

The defendants were Italian, and white Anglo-Saxon Canadian society was still suspicious of olive-skinned "foreigners." On top of that, the victim had been a police officer and a war hero, and courts were not inclined to show mercy to cop-killers. There was a story circulating that Emilio Picariello belonged to a secret Italian Murder Society. The defense lawyer dismissed the story, saying it was absurd and that ". . . no such society exists in this province, and if any such society ever existed, Picariello would be the last Italian in Canada to have anything to do with it." Nonetheless, the story was out there, as was the old tale that Emperor Pic had sent Florence and her husband to work with Italian gangsters in Pennsylvania.

The trial wound up with a four-hour-long plea to the jury. But the effort was in vain. Both Picariello and Florence were found guilty of murder; Florence because she had confessed the crime to Scott, and Emilio because witnesses swore they had heard him tell Florence to shoot the policeman. Both were sentenced to be hanged. As Florence wept, the judge suggested that there was a possibility the government might commute her sentence. Would the government allow a woman to be hanged?

Only four women had suffered the death penalty in Canada since Confederation. Several others had been sentenced to death, but the sentences had been changed to life imprisonment. No woman had gone to the gallows since 1899. Moreover, no woman had ever been hanged in Alberta. Western Canadians, people said, had too much respect for women ever to hang one.

Petitions were made to the governments in Edmonton and Ottawa to spare Florence's life. Other petitions argued that if women were demanding equal rights with men, they should receive the same punishments as men for the same crimes. But Florence clung to the hope that her sentence would be commuted. She and Picariello sweated it out on Death Row in the Fort Saskatchewan prison as the execution date of May 2 crept closer.

Then, days before the black date, Florence made a last ditch attempt to save her own life. She said that she had *not* shot Lawson at all. She claimed that after the shooting, Picariello had told her to "confess." He said that Alberta wouldn't hang a woman, and that after he had been acquitted and she went to prison, he would hire the best lawyers in the province to get her out. Whether or not this story was true, the government did not believe her. There would be no reprieve.

At 5:00 in the morning on May 2, 1923, 47-year-old Emilio Picariello dropped to his death on the Fort Saskatchewan gallows. His last words were: "Why are you hanging an innocent man?"

Less than an hour later Florence Lassandro climbed the steps to the scaffold after a long walk from the women's section of the prison. "Why do you hang me when I didn't do anything?" she pleaded. "Is there no one here who has any pity?"

The executioner silently placed the hood over her head, adjusted the noose around her neck, and pulled the lever, which sprang the trap door. It was 11 minutes before the attending physician pronounced her dead.

The following year the people of Alberta voted to end prohibition in their province. It had caused too much violence and death. Florence Lassandro was the only woman ever hanged in Alberta. Although there was no blockbuster film made about the pistol-packing girl bootlegger, there is an opera about her life. Written by John Estacio and John Murrell, it is called *Filumena* – the name she had as an innocent little girl.

12

Women Pilots of World War II

Eager for the Air

The weather was bad when Marion Orr climbed into the cockpit of a Royal Air Force Spitfire fighter plane. The decision to fly or to wait for the skies to clear was hers alone. This was a trip she had made many times before, delivering planes from an airbase in England to another base in Scotland. She called it her milk run.

Marion decided to take off. Shortly after she rose into the sky and headed the plane north, conditions started to get worse. Rain and low cloud put Marion off course, and soon she was lost. In the early 1940s Britain and her allies were at war with Nazi Germany. Marion was under orders to fly at low altitudes and to keep radio silence. She could not call anyone for help. Even though there wasn't much chance of an enemy fighter spotting her in this soupy sky, there were still many other dangers. Marion could easily wind up like her fellow pilots, the British flyers Jane Winstone and Amy Johnson. Winstone had been killed when her Spitfire crashed, and Johnson was missing and presumed dead after her Oxford trainer had gone down in the sea.

Marion was almost out of fuel when she looked down through the haze and saw a river. She decided to ditch the plane in the water rather than risk crashing into a house. She uttered a quick prayer and started down. At almost the last moment she spotted the orange lights of a runway. She turned away from the river, and guided her plane to the safety of a Royal Air Force airfield. When the ground crew came running out to greet her, one of them said that he knew an Air Transport Auxiliary pilot was flying the plane, because no one else would dare to fly in such bad weather.

Marion Orr of Toronto, Ontario, was one of four Canadian women to fly for the Air Transport Auxiliary (ATA) during World War II. The others, Violet Milstead of Toronto, Helen Harrison of Vancouver, British Columbia, and Elspeth Russell of Matane, Québec, were also skilled pilots. Marion, Violet, and Helen had all tried to join the Royal Canadian Air Force, but were rejected because they were women. Elspeth, who was the youngest and who had lied about her age to join up, did not learn to fly until after the war began.

When war broke out in 1939, Canadian women wanted to do their part along with the tens of thousands of Canadian men who joined the armed forces. Some women took 'men's' jobs in factories. Others joined the women's auxiliaries of the army, navy and air force. But women with specialized abilities, such as those who could fly airplanes, thought they should be able to put their skills to the best use they could. The Canadian military, however, said fighting of any kind was a job for men. The idea of women in the Royal Canadian Air Force was ridiculous. Canadian women actually had been flying since the 1920s, and the whole world had been captivated by female aviators such as the legendary American Amelia Earhart. Nevertheless, women were considered too small and weak, and too highly strung, to be pilots. They couldn't handle the big military planes, the skeptics said. They would "come apart" under the stress of wartime flying.

When Canada became the main training ground for Allied pilots, some Canadian women – Violet Milstead and Helen Harrison, for instance – served as instructors, turning young male recruits into flyers. A few of the students, of course, were not comfortable with the idea of being trained by "little girls," but as far as Helen Harrison was concerned, "Once in the air,

I wasn't male or female; I was an instructor." But even though training pilots was an important contribution to the Allied war effort, these women were frustrated. Men with much less flight experience than they had were being sent to fight in the skies over Britain and Europe. The women's wartime slogan, "We serve that men may fly," just did not satisfy them.

The chance for women pilots to become more involved came with the Air Transport Auxiliary (ATA). This was a British organization whose job was to deliver aircraft of all kinds to bases in Britain and, later in the war, to Europe and Africa. Its pilots wore a uniform similar to that of the RAF. Its motto was *Aetheris Avidi* – Eager for the Air.

Because the RAF needed every available young male pilot for its fighters and bombers, most of the ATA pilots were older men. The young RAF flyers joked that ATA stood for "Ancient and Tattered Aviators." One hundred and sixty-six of the ATA pilots were female, and those women had to fight every step of the way for the right to fly the same aircraft as the men flew. It was only because of a steadily growing need for more pilots that the women were permitted to fly a greater variety of planes.

In spite of the wisecracks of the young male pilots, the ATA performed a vital function. Planes had to be flown from factories to air bases, and from one air base to another as demand required. Damaged aircraft, some of them barely fit to take to the air, had to be flown to locations where they could be repaired or scrapped. Helen Harrison was almost killed delivering an old Lysander reconnaissance plane to the "graveyard." The fact that 154 ATA pilots were killed in the line of duty is proof that the work was dangerous. There was always the threat of enemy aircraft, but the greatest hazards lay in the conditions under which ATA pilots often had to fly.

First, and often the most deadly, was the weather. The frequent fog and rain of the British Isles made flying difficult at the best of times. And wartime precautions meant that ATA pilots had to fly at low altitudes and without the use of radios. Pilots who got lost or encountered other difficulties were on their own. Ships at sea were not allowed to use their radios to report on sudden changes in weather, so a flight that began with good conditions could become a nightmare without warning. Russell, Harrison, Milstead, and Orr all had close calls because of the changeable British weather. As Vi Milstead commented, "You get into difficulties, or, you get yourself into difficulties. You get out of them and there is nothing much to tell. Or you don't get out of them, and someone else does the telling."

Since ATA pilots could not make use of the aircraft's navigational instruments, they had to fly at low altitudes, using maps and compass and getting their bearings from roads and railways. The Canadian pilots, who were used to flying in the wide open spaces of home, found it confusing adjusting to Britain, where everything was crowded and roads and railways ran in every direction like spaghetti. ATA pilots had to keep to specific flight corridors in order to avoid the huge balloons that were sent up to hinder enemy aircraft. If the pilots mistakenly strayed into restricted airspace, their own forces might assume they were enemy planes and shoot them down. Strictly enforced blackouts made night flying all the more difficult.

One of the big attractions of the ATA for pilots – and also one of the complications – was the chance to fly aircraft of many different kinds and Marks. (There were, for example, several different Marks of the Spitfire.) Unlike RAF pilots who trained for just one type of aircraft, ATA pilots had to be able to fly anything the British, and later the Americans, put in the air. A pilot would be tested on one type of aircraft, and then be expected to fly every other Mark in that aircraft's class, even if he or she had never been in one before. ATA pilots flew single-engine, twin-engine, and four-engine planes. They flew everything from fast little fighters to the big Halifax bombers. It was said that there wasn't an Allied plane in the skies over Britain that hadn't been flown at least once by an ATA pilot.

Russell, Harrison, Milstead, and Orr had to contend not only with the many types of aircraft, but also with the alterations that were made to the planes as the war progressed. Engineers were constantly coming up with new ways to improve the speed and maneuverability of warplanes. They had to keep ahead of the *Luftwaffe*, the German air force.

To help the pilots with this incredibly difficult task, there was a book called the Blue Bible. The pilot's "Bible" was a book of small cards, each of which had notes on the operation of a particular plane. Helen Harrison said, "With it you could fly anything. It told us how to inspect the aircraft, the procedures for take-off and landing, how to fly straight and level, and so on. You'd be up there and think, 'Now, how do you land it. Well, I'll look in my Blue Book!'" Once, when an RAF pilot exclaimed to Violet Milstead as she was about to get into a Beaufighter night fighter, "Good God, girl! You can't fly this plane from a book!" She replied, "I can from *my* book."

The pilots liked to say that ATA stood for 'Anything to Anywhere.' But of the 99 different types of aircraft ATA pilots flew, the Spitfire was the one every pilot dreamed of flying. The Spitfire was a winged miracle. It helped turn the tide in the crucial Battle of Britain in 1940, when Nazi forces were poised to invade England. It represented state-of-the-art aviation technology. Marion Orr, recalling her first flight in a Spitfire, recalled, "It was very maneuverable, light, and sensitive . . . I added power and was pressed right back in the seat as I went screaming down the runway, shot off, and was 5,000 feet [1,525 meters] up before I knew it."

Helen Harrison had a different kind of thrill in 1943 when she was returning to England from her leave in Canada. She took off from Montréal as the co-pilot of a Mitchell bomber. "I was happy as a lark and higher than a kite," she said later. Helen was the only Canadian woman to ferry a military aircraft across the Atlantic during World War II. "The most difficult part of the flight was using the tube to go to the bathroom," she recalled. "I got a little damp. The captain and I had a good laugh about that."

The women of the ATA had to make an extra effort to excel just because they were female in what was considered male territory. If they made a mistake, someone was bound to say, "I told you so." Women had to undergo longer training than men. Male pilots had to make four successful solo landings in a Halifax bomber to qualify for four-engined planes. Women were required to make *10*! Female pilots who were of small stature, like Elspeth Russell, had to find ways to compensate so they could handle the controls in cockpits that were designed for bigger people. Elspeth never allowed her size to be a problem. Her commanding officer reported: "An excellent ferry pilot in her Class. Hardworking and ready for any job allotted to her." Statistics compiled after the war showed that the women pilots of the ATA actually had a better safety record than the men.

When the war ended in 1945, the ATA was disbanded. Because it was a civilian organization, although run along military lines, there were no medals or ceremonies for its flyers, even though they had performed a vital service so courageously.

Eventually Marion Orr and Helen Harrison were inducted into Canada's Aviation Hall of Fame, and Marion received the Order of Canada. All of the Canadian women who had flown with the ATA helped female pilots to become accepted in Canada – often in the face of stubborn opposition. They could look back with pride to the war years when they had climbed into the cockpits of fighter planes and bombers, and dared to challenge the notion that women should not fly.

Further Reading

Black, Martha, *My Seventy Years*, Thomas Nelson & Sons, Toronto, 1938

Horan, James D., *Desperate Women*, Bonanza Books, New York, 1962

Hubbard, Mina, *A Woman's Way Through Unknown Labrador*, Breakwater Books, St. John's NF, 1981 (original in 1908)

Johnston, Jean, *Wilderness Women*, Peter Martin Ass. Ltd., Toronto, 1973

MacEwan, Grant, *And Mighty Women, Too*, Western Producer Prairie Books, Saskatoon, SK, 1975

Merritt, Susan, *Her Story: Women From Canada's Past*, Vanwell Publishing, St. Catharines, ON, 1993

Render, Shirley, *No Place For a Lady: The Story of Canadian Women Pilots 1928-1992*, Portage & Main Press, Winnipeg, 1992

Robinson, Helen Caistor, *Mistress Molly*, Dundurn Press, Toronto, 1980

Sadlier, Rosemary, *Mary Ann Shadd*, Umbrella Press, Toronto, 1995

Spring, Joyce, *Daring Lady Flyers*, Pottersfield Press, East Lawrencetown, NS, 1994

Van Kirk, Sylvia, *Many Tender Ties*, Watson & Dwyer, Winnipeg, 1980